The Kingtons

Dedicated to my father
Chris Ryland, with love

The Kingtons

a History of the Ancient Parish of Kington

St Michael with Kington Langley

Louise Ryland-Epton

First published in the United Kingdom in 2024

by The Hobnob Press,
8 Lock Warehouse, Severn Road, Gloucester GL1 2GA
www.hobnobpress.co.uk

in association with Kington St Michael Parish Council and the Victoria County History of England.

VICTORIA COUNTY HISTORY is the registered trade mark ® of the Institute of Historical Research, School of Advanced Study, University of London.

British Library Cataloguing in Publication Data
A catalogue record for this book is available from the British Library

ISBN 978-1-914407-69-7

Typeset in Chaparral Pro, 11/14 pt
Typesetting and origination by John Chandler

front cover based on original artwork by John Harris
back cover 'The Old Thorn' etching by Robin Tanner (Wiltshire Museum 1986.522)

Contents

   *considers the topography of the villages of Kington St Michael and
   Kington Langley, their physical characteristics, and the settlements'
   development over time. Case studies examine Langley Fitzurse and
   Easton Piercy, two hamlets within the larger villages that have
   intriguing histories of their own. Another case study looks at the
   antiquaries and historians who have lived or had associations with
   the villages from the 17th to the 20th centuries.*

   *looks at how those living in the communities of Kington St Michael
   and Kington Langley made their living, particularly agriculture
   and textiles. Case studies explain the dramatic impact of the Black
   Death, and, alongside a consideration of the economic influence of
   women, another examines the life of a local alehouse keeper, Edith
   Brown.*

   *examines local crimes throughout the centuries and how many of
   them were dealt with within the communities of Kington St Michael
   and Kington Langley, including their punishments – the gallows,
   stocks and cucking stool. A case study looks at the 1822 Langley
   revel which ended in two deaths. The chapter also considers how
   the villages managed their affairs and, in two case studies, how the
   villages met the demands of World War Two.*

Preface

One of the most famous sons of Kington St Michael, John Britton, planned to write a history of the place of his birth. To that end, he commissioned a map and engravings of the church and assembled 'ample materials' to use in its production. In June 1845 he anticipated no difficulty in getting the whole thing published by the following winter. However, it was not to be; distracted by other projects, ill health, old age and money worries [evidently the inhabitants of Kington had not been 'sufficiently liberal and enlightened to encourage such a work'] it was never completed. Instead, the map, engravings, and Britton's 'ample materials' – his notes, correspondence and more were deposited at the Wiltshire Museum in Devizes.

Almost 180 years later I began researching the history of the Kingtons and had the pleasure of consulting Britton's work. Like Britton, my journey has also had its distractions, but my distractions were happily almost entirely limited to a surfeit of delights that I found in Britton and the papers of two other antiquaries who wrote about the villages. These sent me down rabbit holes and kept me up late into the night.

The first was Canon John Edward Jackson, whose history of Kington St Michael, which included Kington Langley, was published in 1858. Jackson's notes, which include his drawings, anecdotes, newspaper clippings, photographs and much more, are in the Society of Antiquaries of London. I spent several happy days in their library exploring these among his voluminous scrapbooks created over a long lifetime with material on many Wiltshire parishes. I hope that they will be made available to the broader public in years to come. They are a treasure trove.

Finally, I have used the manuscripts of the incomparable 17th-century native of Kington St Michael, John Aubrey. Those who know me are aware that I am slightly obsessed with Aubrey's life and work. In writing this book, I have lost entire days reading and rereading his manuscripts and marvelling over his drawings. His writings and sublime pictures do much to elevate this text.

In thinking about the text, I must pay credit to my VCH collaborator, Mark Forrest, who has set me on a trail of exciting anecdotes. Along with John Chandler he has corrected my occasional erroneous readings of the medieval source material and acted as a repository of knowledge. This book began with the work that Mark and I were contracted to do by Wiltshire Victoria County History Trust. In starting our research into the Kingtons, VCH supporter Tim Couzens introduced us to Colin Labouchere, a stalwart of Kington St Michael life, who arranged for me to talk in the village hall about the VCH and some of our early findings. Inspired by Colin's infectious enthusiasm, we explored the prospect of creating a 'not dull' history book about Kington St Michael alongside the VCH draft. I am delighted that Wiltshire VCH Trust allowed me to use our research, and Gerry Gamble and Kington St Michael parish council commissioned the work. Later, another talk at Kington Langley was the catalyst for the history of that parish, once part of Kington St Michael, to be incorporated into the text. For this I am indebted to Edward Buchan.

This volume has been produced in partnership with the Victoria County History project, which has created meticulous placed-based histories for over a century, and Hobnob Press, which has published local histories for 40 years. I am particularly obliged to Catherine Clarke of the VCH and John Chandler of Hobnob for their support.

The following text is structured as a thematic history of Kington St Michael and Kington Langley. Each chapter explores a different aspect of the villages' past. Within these thematic chapters I have included detailed case studies, highlighting some of the most significant events and individuals that shaped the history of the Kingtons. The book is based on primary source material, and although not footnoted like a VCH volume, I have provided a bibliography. Further details can be found in the forthcoming Wiltshire VCH volume.

Acknowledgements

Tim Storer for sharing his local knowledge, reading this text and for allowing me to use his collection of photographs and postcards.

Tim Couzens for his support, research, and local knowledge.

Mark Forrest my VCH partner in crime and god of all things manorial history.

John Chandler my VCH and Hobnob partner. The best editor and mentor I could hope for.

John Harris for the wonderful cover illustration.

Colin Labouchere who got the whole thing started.

Edward Buchan for his meticulous reading or the text, helpful comments, but particularly for his facilitating the inclusion of Kington Langley into the text.

Viv Vines and Gerry Gamble, and members of the Kington St Michael Parish Council for their support.

Kington Langley villagers who in 2016 generously helped raise funds for research and writing their chapter in *VCH Wiltshire* vol. XX, and thenceforwards Kington Langley Scarecrows Festival and the Parish Council

Betty Bird who kindly shared her memories of Kington Langley with me.

Paul and Carolyn Gilman.

Jane Schon and Wiltshire Museum.

Mel Barnett and Chippenham Museum.

The Bodleian Library for permission to use illustrations from the manuscripts of John Aubrey in my text.

The Society of Antiquaries of London.

Catherine Clarke and Ruth Slatter of Victoria County History central office at the Institute of Historical Research.

James Holden and Trustees of the Wiltshire Victoria County History Trust.

Helen Taylor, Ian Hicks and Julie Davies at Wiltshire and Swindon History Centre.

The Friday regulars at the Three Crowns in Chippenham.

And last but not least to my wonderful family Mike, Loren, Poppy and Lucky.

This map is a redrawn and simplified version of the map made for John Britton in 1842 and illustrated on pages 34–35. It depicts some of the principal buildings and sites described in this book.

A reissued copy of the 1828 Ordnance Survey map of the Chippenham area showing the position of Kington St Michael and Kington Langley within their north Wiltshire surroundings.

Estate map of Edward Coleman in Kington Langley 1770.
Reproduced courtesy of the Wiltshire and Swindon History
Centre, Chippenham, 873.141L.

1
LOCATION, LANDSCAPE AND LEGEND

THOUSANDS OF PEOPLE travel daily along the dual carriageway road, which leads to the motorway and divides Kington St Michael to the west and Kington Langley to the east. Millions more each year unwittingly follow the northern boundaries of both parishes as they drive at speed along the motorway itself. Most of these travellers take this landscape for granted, and few will ever visit the two villages, nor take time to explore the pleasant countryside that makes up their territory and the attractive stone houses clustered and scattered about it. But before we delve into the details of our two communities' history, we should examine their setting and try to understand how they have come to be as they are.

Until 1866, when it was broken up, there was a single parish of Kington St Michael. It included Kington Langley and also Easton Piercy, which lies further west. This block of almost 4,000 acres of rural north Wiltshire extended some four miles east to west close to Chippenham. As an economic unit this territory was very ancient, as its boundaries seem to have been described in a Saxon charter of 940 AD; it did not then include Easton Piercy, but Draycot Cerne may then have been a part. Soon thereafter, it came into the possession of Glastonbury abbey, who retained it for more than five centuries. Easton Piercy never belonged

View southeast from Easton Piercy towards Kington St Michael by John Aubrey c.1670. Reproduced courtesy of the Bodleian Libraries, University of Oxford, MSS Aubrey 3, fol 60r.

to Glastonbury, but it was included when the parish was created and so became one of the three portions, known as tithings, into which the parish was divided, along with Kington Langley and Kington St Michael itself.

Much of the ancient parish boundary remains, following watercourses, old routeways such as Jacksom's Lane, or running in fairly straight alignments between later enclosed fields. In places it has been modified by later developments, such as the M4 motorway, so that the Leigh Delamere services is now bisected by it. Another feature which Kington shared with its neighbours was that, until boundaries were rationalised in the 19th century, it possessed various small detached portions of land away from the main block and surrounded by other parishes. This, it would appear, came about so that the community had sufficient meadowland for its needs, or in some cases, as at Peckingell on the River Avon, a source of water-power for a mill.

This part of Wiltshire borders the Gloucestershire Cotswolds and shares some of its characteristics, although on a gentler scale.

The trees of Easton Piercy sketch dated 12 April 1670 by John Aubrey. Reproduced courtesy of the Bodleian Libraries, University of Oxford, is MSS Aubrey 17 fol.9r

The underlying limestone rocks, known as Cornbrash and Forest Marble, can be and have been used as building stone, though not of the finest quality. Along the south of the parish, and in a few places elsewhere, the limestone is overlain by a heavy clay, named Kellaways after a nearby hamlet where it prevails. This geology has created an undulating landscape, with soils rich in lime but heavy and poorly drained in places, and more suitable as pasture for dairying and cattle rearing than for growing crops. Apart from Heywood, south of Kington St Michael, there is little woodland in the parish, but that was probably not always the case. The name 'Langley', shared with Langley Burrell nearby, implies a long area of woodland or wood-pasture partly cleared for settlement and farming in the Saxon period. In that case it may have been a continuation of the wooded forests of Selwood, Melksham and Chippenham further south and east, and Bradon forest to the north.

Woodland clearance during the 17th century was mourned by the scientist and naturalist John Aubrey, a native of the parish who will feature frequently throughout this history. Aubrey was aware of the changing landscapes around his childhood home at Kington St

Michael, remarking on the impact of enclosure and deforestation or 'disafforestations'. But he celebrated the fine surviving oak woodland at Easton Piercy. His anecdotes on soil, plants, birds, insects, reptiles and more are beautifully observed. On the pine marten, he wrote, 'upon these disafforestations the marterns were utterly destroyed in North Wilts. It is a pretty little beast and of a deep chesnutt colour, a kind of polecat, lesse than a fox; and the furrre is much esteemed.' At Kington he noted that wormwood grew plentifully alongside 'Worm-wax (*Luteola*), my Lady's bed-straw, sorrell and abundance of Sowre-herbes. Hartstongue, Adders-tongue, Mayden-hair, Brook lime. It is an excellent place for Plants.' In the old hedges around the lands of the former priory in the parish there were a great number of 'berberry-trees' which 'I suppose the nunnes made use of for confections.' Nature was a passion, and while recording the flora around the former priory, he observed, 'there is infinite variety of plants; and it would have tempted me to have been a botanist had I had the leisure . . .'

The earliest evidence of human activity in this wooded environment are stray finds of flint implements used by Mesolithic hunters and fishers. In the Neolithic period, from about 3,500 BC, and later through the Bronze and Iron ages, people settled and farmed the area, and have left slight traces of their activities. Cropmarks of enclosures have been recognised east of the later village and near Nash Lane further north, and the ring ditch of a possible burial mound was seen on an aerial photograph near the main A350 road. Settlement in the area continued through the Iron age into the Romano-British period, with evidence

Collection of finds made by Tim Storer in Kington St Michael.

of farmsteads near Heywood and Cromhall, west of Kington St Michael, Courtfields north of Langley Fitzurse, and elsewhere. Such clues and traces from the distant past are typical of north Wiltshire, and indeed of much of lowland England – the 'background noise' underlying more recent settlement patterns.

What is unusual about the Kingtons is their place in the history of studying places. Two pioneering scholars of antiquarian research, John Aubrey in the 17th century and John Britton in the 19th, were born here and wrote about their native parish. Canon John Jackson, the most important Wiltshire historian working in the Victorian era, was minister at Leigh Delamere nearby, and published a detailed history of Kington St Michael. Then in the 20th century Heather Tanner, with her artist husband Robin, wrote extensively about this area of north Wiltshire, centred on their home in Kington Langley.

Kington St Michael as drawn by John Britton. Reproduced courtesy of the Society of Antiquaries, London, JAC 006.

Case Study: Antiquaries and Historians

ACCORDING to the 19th-century antiquary John Britton, 'No topographical work can be deemed complete without authentic accounts of those persons who, by their acts and deeds, their genius and talents, or any other qualities, whether of good or evil have conferred notoriety upon the locality referred to, either as a place of their birth or temporary abode.' Thus, by his standards, no account of Kington St Michael would be complete without an account of Britton himself, who was born in the village in 1771. Before his death Britton was anxious that his name should not be forgotten in Kington and was planning ways in which it would be perpetuated. Sadly, he died before articulating what his plans were. Britton never completed a planned history of the village, but he did publish a biographical work on the other famous antiquary from the parish, John Aubrey, who was born there in 1626. After Britton's death, he and Aubrey were memorialised in glass in

n to J.E.Jackson,

John Aubrey. (2024, February 17).
In public domain via Wikimedia
commons.

the parish church at the instigation of yet another antiquary with close ties to Kington, John Jackson of Leigh Delamere, who published his own history of Kington in 1858. In the 20th century Heather and Robin Tanner became fascinated by the landscape around their home in Kington Langley.

John Aubrey

By his own account, Aubrey was born 'very weak and like to dye' at Lower Easton Piercy in Kington St Michael in 1626. He survived infancy but was a sickly child. As an adult, he continued to cheat death. He survived smallpox. He was shipwrecked in 1660, and in 1664 suffered a 'terrible fit of the spleen and piles' while on the continent. The same year, Aubrey endured an injury to his genitalia 'which was like to have been fatal.' In 1666, he spent a year 'under an ill tongue', probably believing a witch had cursed him. Added to this, he was almost drowned twice; was nearly murdered by the Earl of Pembroke in 1669; 'in danger' of 'being run through with a sword' by a lawyer while a guest of Mr Burges at Middle Temple in 1673; and nearly 'killed by a drunkard in the street of Gray's Inn by a gentleman whom I never saw before'. Aubrey also had the misfortune to live through one of the most tumultuous periods in English history, the Civil Wars. Although he was on the sidelines, the war disrupted his education, and he watched, with

A small landscape of Kington St Michael made by John Aubrey at the end of one of his manuscripts. Reproduced courtesy of the Bodleian Libraries, University of Oxford, MSS Aubrey 17, fol 20r.

some sadness, the world changing around him. Aubrey was unlucky
in his relationships too. He lost large sums of money in lawsuits from
several disgruntled suitors and ultimately, in 1670, was forced to sell the
family estate at Lower Easton Piercy in Kington St Michael, which he
had inherited from his father already debt-ridden in 1652. Despite these
tribulations, Aubrey remained philosophical, grateful to many friends who
supported him in his straitened circumstances. He is characterised as
charming, warm and popular, but was ill-disposed to business preferring a
life of 'literary ease'.

The best known of his literary works are his biographical notes.
Brief Lives is considered a classic of English literature. Aubrey was on
friendly terms with many of the greatest minds and artists of his day –
Sir Isaac Newton, Edmond Halley, Christopher Wren, Thomas Hobbes,
John Evelyn and many more, including Charles II who commissioned
him to write a work. Aubrey was an early fellow of the Royal Society.
Within Wiltshire Aubrey's significance lies in his investigations of natural
history, topography, and antiquities. He was one of the first, if not the
first, English archaeologists, notable for his work on Avebury stone circle.
These interests began in his childhood, and consequently anecdotes and
sketches of Kington St Michael pepper his manuscripts. He described the
oak tree growing by his dairy as being the biggest one in the county and
the stones around his childhood home 'full of very small cockles' but also
'blewish' and 'dampish and sweate, and doe emit a cold and unwholesome
dampe.' Although sadly none of his local work was published during his
lifetime some of the images Aubrey made of Easton Piercy and Kington St
Michael appear in this book.

Aubrey was superstitious. Although sometimes derided later for
his beliefs and writings on the supernatural, it is as well to remember that
such beliefs were characteristic of the times and shared by many of his
contemporaries, including fellow members of the Royal Society. Aubrey
was also not naïve. In writing about phantoms, for example, he wrote 'I
believe that extraordinarily there have been such apparitions; but where
one is true a hundred are figments.'

Aubrey died in 1697, and though his intellectual standing
subsequently slipped, his fellow Kington-born antiquary, Britton, helped to
rescue his posthumous reputation during the 19th century.

John Britton

John Britton was more ambiguous in his feelings for his native village, Kington St Michael, than John Aubrey. He was born in Kington, of humble origins, a stone's throw from St Michael's church where he was baptised on August 4 1771 in relatively humble origins. He spent his early childhood in the village in the 1770s and early 1780s. In old age, he wrote of this period 'a full fifteen years were wasted and frittered away in trifling miscellaneous occupation, and in learning words and things which were almost wholly useless.' At 15, he left the village, which he found quiet and dull, and was apprenticed in London. He spent years studying secretly after working in the cellar of a tavern. A chance encounter with Edward Wedlake Brayley, a future literary collaborator, changed Britton's life. He consequently published two volumes on the topography of the county of his birth, *The Beauties of Wiltshire*, in 1801. Volumes of *The Beauties of England and Wales* came

The childhood home of John Britton at Kington St Michael, by J Walmsley. Reproduced courtesy of the Society of Antiquaries, London, JAC 006.

next and were followed by *The Architectural Antiquities of Great Britain*. His crowning work, however, was probably the *Cathedral Antiquities of England* published in fourteen volumes between 1814 and 1835. These sumptuously produced books with their meticulous plans and elevations have been described as 'among the greatest … glories of British book design.'

A workaholic during most of his adult life, Britton published little in his last few years, save his *Autobiography* and *Memoir of John Aubrey*. During this period, however, he reconnected with the village of his youth. His fellow antiquary, John Jackson, noted: 'In the year 1848, Mr Britton being at Chippenham for the meeting of the Wilts Society came to visit me at Leigh Delamere. He had not been at his native place, Kington for 40 years. As I was driving him to the village, he became very silent, as we approached his birthplace he lifted up his hands and said "What a

Portrait of John Britton in 1845 by John Wood. (2024, February 13). In public domain via Wikimedia commons.

hole!'" Despite these feelings, likely to have been expressed towards his childhood home rather than the village itself, Britton planned a history of the village, noting 'though the parish is comparatively unimportant, and almost unnoticed in the annals of Topography, it possesses characteristics entitling it to a separate history.' He made several sketches of sites in the village. However, he became frustrated by the lack of interest shown in the endeavour, including from those within the village. He noted in his *Autobiography* 'My topographical collections for Kington are extensive, and have cost me much time and money, but it would be improper and improvident for me to appropriate more of either, without a reasonable prospect of some reward.' The book was eventually shelved.

Although Britton never published his history of Kington St Michael, in 1847 he edited and published one of John Aubrey's manuscripts as the *Natural History of Wiltshire*. It included numerous anecdotes about the village. While Britton had intended to publish the manuscript in full, 'after mature deliberation it has been thought more desirable to select only such passages as directly or indirectly apply to the county of Wilts, or which comprise information really useful or interesting in itself, or curious as illustrating the state of literature and science at the time when they were written.' It was thus only a partial edition. Britton's edits of Aubrey's text included removing an entire chapter on Aubrey's hypothesis of the 'terraqueous globe' where Aubrey [rightly] conjectured that the world was older than had previously been believed and had been once covered in water.

After 1848 Britton returned sporadically to Kington, including in 1853 to show Mrs Britton 'my native place and the humble home of my birth.' He died in 1857.

John Jackson

John Edward Jackson was born in 1805 and, after taking his degree at Oxford, became a Church of England minister. From 1845 until he died in 1891 he was the rector of the small parish of Leigh Delamere, adjacent to Kington St Michael, and lived as a bachelor clergyman in the rectory there. Jackson was fascinated by the antiquities and history of Wiltshire and spent much of his time researching and writing about his adopted county, especially the places around him. Like Britton, Jackson was influenced by Aubrey and published a greatly expanded version of Aubrey's collection of notes on Wiltshire. He also wrote a history of the Kingtons, published in 1858. And, like Aubrey and Britton before him, Jackson made sketches of the village, but also took or commissioned some of its earliest photographs. He was one of the founders of the Wiltshire Archaeological and Natural History Society and the editor of its journal. He was made an honorary canon of Bristol cathedral, and was generally referred to in later life as 'the dear old Canon'. When he died, his friends and colleagues recognised him as pre-eminent among the county's historians and a worthy successor to Aubrey and Britton.

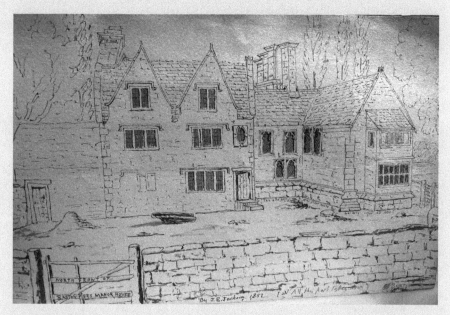

Easton Piercy by John Jackson in 1851. Reproduced courtesy of the Society of Antiquaries, London, JAC 006.

Heather and Robin Tanner

Heather Spackman was a grocer's daughter and grew up in Corsham, where she had been born in 1903. At Chippenham Grammar School, she met and fell in love with a fellow-pupil, Robin Tanner, a budding artist, and eventually, in 1931, they married. As a wedding present an architect uncle designed and built them a house, in Arts & Crafts style, Old Chapel Field in Kington Langley. They lived a contented life there until he died in 1988 and she in 1993. They were Quakers and pacifists, deeply interested in the history and natural history around them. Besides his day-job as a school inspector, Robin was an artist and etcher. During the 1930s, Heather wrote *Wiltshire Village*, which Robin illustrated with line drawings and etchings. It was published in 1939 and is an elegy of country life between the wars. The imagined village they portrayed, which they called Kington Borel, was an amalgamation of the Kingtons, Langley Burrell, and all the nearby north-west Wiltshire countryside within about a ten-mile radius of their home. They collaborated on further books on woodland plants and country lore, and Robin wrote an autobiography describing their life together. They were forthright supporters of ecological and human rights organisations, and Heather became an anti-nuclear campaigner protesting at Greenham Common and RAF Fairford. A collection of her writings, *An Exceptional Woman*, was published in 2006.

The Wicket Gate and October by Robin Tanner.
Both images are derived from Robin's sketches of Kington Langley. Reproduced courtesy of Wiltshire Museum, Devizes, 1986.525, 1986.535.

If the name 'Langley' helps us to understand the history of the place, so too does the name 'Kington', which means 'the king's farm'. By the 9th century, Chippenham was a large royal estate responsible for accommodating the king and his entourage when required. At this time the Anglo Saxon monarchs were peripatetic. The Kington part of

the Chippenham estate seems to have been the home farm, supplying produce for the royal household. Easton Piercy was not part of the estate, but its name, too, is indicative. It was the farm on the eastern side of Yatton Keynell, with which it was initially associated. 'Piercy', like 'Keynell' and Langley 'Fitzurse' and 'Burrell', were names adopted later, and denote the names of the medieval families who owned the estates. 'St Michael' refers to Kington's church dedication, but for a time it had two other names, Kington Monachorum ('of the monks') referring to Glastonbury abbey, and *Minchinkinton* ('Kington of the nuns'), because a priory for nuns was established on the edge of the village before 1155. The name 'Swinley', a farm in the north of the parish near the motorway, may also tell us about its origin as a woodland clearance for rearing pigs.

The Kington territory, as defined by the Saxons, had become, through the medieval centuries, a land of scattered farms and three principal foci of settlement. Two of these, Easton Piercy and Langley Fitzurse, are the subjects of separate case studies. The third, Kington St Michael, was the most important. It had the parish church, built here in the 12th century or earlier, and it was here that Glastonbury abbey established its headquarters – its grange – for administering the Kington estate. There would have been a village too, but perhaps not where it is now. Archaeological evidence suggests that there were buildings further south, towards Tor Hill, which only survive as the slight earthworks of house platforms.

Shifting medieval settlements are not uncommon, and the likely context is a decision by Glastonbury in the 13th century to try to develop Kington into a small town. In 1266, the abbot was given leave to establish a weekly Tuesday market and an annual September fair. Over the next few decades, the abbey also enlarged the church, added a steeple, and built itself a new grange. And for a time the North Damerham hundred court, which administered justice over the nearby parishes, was held here. Glastonbury's ambition for Kington may still be seen behind the present High Street, where the properties run back to a continuous rear boundary, often indicating medieval town planning. It would have intended to urbanise the village by attracting craftsmen and traders to take up the plots, which were thus created for their homes and workshops.

If this was the intention, it was bound to fail. The expansive era of new town creation was ended around 1300 by epidemics and falling population, and Kington was too close to the established market town of Chippenham to compete. The market may have continued, as Aubrey, in the 17th century, recalled that it was held at the cross located at the 'Y going to the Priory', which would be the junction of Grove Lane and Honey Knob Hill. However, more important to Kington's economy was the existence of the priory. St Mary's priory had been established by 1155 north-west of the village as a Benedictine house for nuns. Its buildings surrounded a square court, with a chapel to the north, which survived largely intact in the 17th century. Although a small establishment, as a local landowner, influencer and employer it must have been very significant.

The most enigmatic settlement in Kington St Michael was Langley Fitzurse. It has largely vanished and been forgotten, but its history is inextricably bound up with the way in which Kington Langley developed as a settlement around its common.

Case Study: Langley Fitzurse

L ANGLEY FITZURSE was a small manor carved from the Langley estate
of Glastonbury abbey by 1086. It comprised approximately 300 acres
and extended from the north side of Parker's Lane northwards from
the present common towards Swinley. Fitzurse was surrounded by the
lands of the abbey. Its holder was the Norman, Urso. His name meant
bear. 'Fitzurse' means son of Urse or Urso, and Fitzurse subsequently
became the name by which the family was known. Urso also held land
from the abbey at nearby Grittleton. An Urso, possibly the same man, was
also recorded in the Domesday Book as the lord of five other places in
Wiltshire and Dorset, including *Chenebuild* in Wiltshire, a place which has
not been identified.

*The medieval barn, all that remained of Fitzurse Manor by the 1950s. reproduced
courtesy of Wiltshire and Swindon History Centre, Chippenham, 2042/34.*

By 1166 the family property in Langley was in the possession of
Reginald Fitzurse, son of Richard Fitzurse. Reginald was probably the

Reginald Fitzurse (with a bear on his shield and sword drawn) at the assassination of Thomas Becket. In public domain via Wikmedia commons.

grandson of the Norman Urso. The family estates had been much enlarged since Domesday with manors in Somerset, Leicestershire, and Northamptonshire. Fitzurse was probably one of his smaller and less important manors, and what acquaintance or association Reginald had with it is unknown. It is not certain that the name 'Fitzurse' was yet attached with this area of Langley, as associations with later members of the family were much closer.

However, close-ties or not with Langley Fitzurse, Reginald has gone down in history as one of the four assassins of Thomas Becket, the archbishop of Canterbury, in December 1170. In the aftermath, Reginald and his companions were excommunicated and fled, taking shelter at Knaresborough before giving themselves up to the King, who sent them to the Pope. Reginald was banished and died in the Holy Land in 1173.

After the death of Reginald, the Fitzurse estate in Langley was left to his daughter, Maud. Thereafter the descent of the family becomes obscure. Maud married Robert Courtney. After their death most of Maud's property passed to her three married aunts (Reginald's sisters). As these women had adopted their husband's name so, by 1221, when the estate next appears in documentary evidence, we would expect it to be in the name of another family. Instead, its holder was a Jordan Fitzurse. This means the estate probably either passed to a cadet branch of the family who had the name Fitzurse, or one of the heirs of Reginald's sisters changed their name to Fitzurse, or that the manor had been sold to a local who adopted Fitzurse as their surname. In this period many surnames were derived from an individual's place of origin.

Thus, we may never know what association Jordan Fitzurse or later
members of the Fitzurse family had with Reginald or indeed if they had
any.

Whether he was a blood relative to Reginald or not, Jordan
Fitzurse has been characterised as having a similar contempt for the
church. The owners of the estate were obliged to pay a regular fee,
essentially a military tax, to Glastonbury abbey called a scutage. However,
Jordan Fitzurse resisted paying this tax, attempting independence from
the influence of the abbey. He failed, but the dispute was not resolved
until 1243. Later relations may have been better as Glastonbury was
granted land from the estate. During the Black Death in the 14th century
members of the family acted as pledges for landless inhabitants, aiding the
community in a time of intense social and economic distress and helping
it to remain a viable one.

By the 16th century, if not before, the c. 300 acre estate was being
called Langley Fitzurse. Tenants of both Glastonbury abbey and Langley
Fitzurse grazed livestock on the common which was then hundreds of
acres (it is now 30 acres). Unsurprisingly 'Langley Fitzurse' was sometimes
also used as a name for the settlement that grew around the common.
The present 19th-century parish church of Kington Langley stands on
land formerly part of Fitzurse, and, somewhat predictably, when the civil
parish was created a few years later many believed it should have been
called Langley Fitzurse and not Kington Langley.

After Glastonbury abbey was dissolved in 1539, Fitzurse was
surrounded by the estate of the Snell family who had bought up Kington
manor. The Fitzurse family were by then no longer resident. The estate
was bought by Owen Hopton in 1566-7, whose descendants retained
it for almost a century before selling it to Bampfield Sydenham. His
descendants, thereafter, held it until the 19th century.

Aubrey described Fitzurse manor house in about 1670 as 'a
very ancient-built house, with a great hall and moated about', but by
1858 it was described as 'now an ordinary house on the village green.'
Neither Aubrey, nor the later antiquaries John Jackson and John Britton
sketched the manor, despite immortalising other local buildings in the
area. And unfortunately, no image of the building has been located.
However, we do know that the manor house was sited slightly north of
Parker's Lane, and that in the 19th century it was an L-shaped building

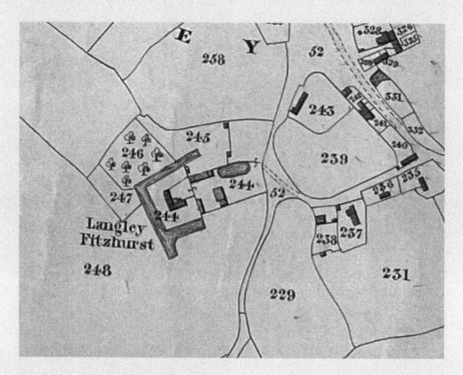

Langley Fitzurse in 1842 with three sides of the moat still visible around the house. Reproduced courtesy of Wiltshire and Swindon History Centre, Chippenham, T/A Kington St Michael.

with eastern and northern ranges, and enclosed on three sides by the remains of a moat. In 1855, 'an ancient sword' inlaid with silver that had been found in the moat was displayed at a temporary exhibition in Chippenham. The whereabouts of this sword is now unknown, and unfortunately no drawing or photograph was made, thus, like the house itself we are reliant on our imagination or artists' impressions.

By the 1850s the Fitzurse estate was much reduced and the manor house and associated buildings were in severe decline. The manor house was described in 1865 as an 'old dilapidated farm house and buildings not worth doing any but slight repairs to.' Another assessment in the same year suggested that a gentleman 'fond of sporting' could use the site to erect a new residence. Instead, however, the site and outbuildings were used for sawmills in the late 19th century. The moat was still visible in the 1930s, by which time the house had been demolished. A medieval barn remained, and the local vicar Canon W J Meers joined efforts to renovate its structure and use it for another purpose. However, efforts failed, and the site was developed for housing in the later 20th century.

Traditions and legends have surrounded Fitzurse for hundreds of years. One recorded by John Aubrey in the 17th century held that 'a king lived here'. There is no evidence yet discovered to support this hypothesis. Aubrey himself conjectured that the Anglo-Saxon king Æthelred had resided within the village of Kington St Michael. Centuries later, in 1841, possibly fusing the two traditions, Walter Coleman wrote to another antiquary, John Britton, that there was 'no doubt' that Æthelred had lived at Fitzurse. However, by Æthelred's reign between 978 and 1016 Langley (and therefore Fitzurse) had already been gifted by the crown to the abbey of Glastonbury. An earlier royal residence at Fitzurse is also unlikely as there was a royal residence at Chippenham between 853 until at least 940.

Other legends are associated with Reginald Fitzurse. These include that Kington Langley did not have a church until the present parish church was built in 1855, as a punishment to the community for the sins of Reginald. This is incorrect, as a chapel was in use at Langley by 1171, although in 1189 it was noted that religious services had been disrupted for an unspecified reason and local people were unhappy. Another tradition held that the annual village celebration, the Langley 'revel', was bound up with the killing of Becket. This too is a myth, as the revel was traditionally celebrated on the Sunday following the feast of St Peter (29 June) and undoubtedly related to the dedication of the chapel. Later the revel appears to have been celebrated on the Sunday after 6 July. In notes by Canon Meers, who wrote a history of the parish in the 1930s, he suggested that it could have been associated with the canonization of Becket which took place in July 1174. However, he does not account for the earlier festivities taking place following 29 June. Although there may not be a sound historical basis to these tales and legends surrounding Fitzurse, the presence of the estate has helped to cement the independence of Langley Fitzurse/ Kington Langley within the ancient parish of Kington St Michael, and it remains an intriguing part of the early history of Kington Langley.

Greathouse (now Kin House) shortly after its renovation and extension in 1913.
Reproduced courtesy of Chippenham Museum, 2009.42.

Whereas Kington St Michael is a close-knit village crowded around its church, almshouses and built-up street – nucleated, to use the geographer's term – Kington Langley is looser and more scattered – 'dispersed' describes such a settlement. It meanders along its three interconnected roads (Plough Lane, the Common and Church Road) and surrounds the linked Lower, Middle and Upper Commons. This character is largely the result of 18th- and 19th-century piecemeal cottage-building, at a time of rapid population growth. In places it overlies an earlier village, as earthworks of house plots are visible on aerial photographs near Silver

The Firs and Upper Common (above) and the Manor House, Kington Langley seen from Greathouse (opposite) in the mid- 20th century. From the collection of Tim Storer.

Street and north of Church Road. The medieval chapel, believed to have stood nearby, must have been a focus of community life.

As the high-status, moated manor house of Fitzurse declined, so others were built to replace it. Greathouse (now renamed Kin House) overlooking the Swindon road, was built in about 1691 for the squire, William Coleman, and was used as the manor house before it was repurposed in the 18th century and later became dilapidated. Its

replacement by the Colemans was a former inn of about 1700, which they took over in 1829 and is now the manor house on Lower Common. The Firs on Upper Common is reputed to date from 1695 but was much altered in the 19th century. Then, as the common-edge village developed, chapels, a school and a parish church were built, and the rough old common began to be described as the 'perfection of a village green'. After Glastonbury abbey was suppressed in 1539, the abbey's grange located in Kington St Michael was used as the manor house. But it was soon rebuilt by Nicholas Snell who acquired the estate. Formal gardens were laid out, and they were visible on an 18th-century map. However, only a small part of the garden survives now. In the 1860s, the manor house was replaced by Herbert Prodgers soon after he aquired it. Aubrey mentioned a park adjacent to the manor that included carp ponds, which may have been a deer park where the abbot's tenants enjoyed the right of pasture. However, these rights were later revoked by Nicholas Snell, although evidence suggests that villagers, despite trespassing, continued to try and enjoy the grounds for centuries. In the 18th century Britton enjoyed fishing and baiting carp in the manor ponds as a boy when they

The old manor house (above) at Kington St Michael the year of its demolition in 1863 and the brand-new manor house (below) in 1864. Photographs taken by or for John Jackson. Reproduced courtesy of Society of Antiquaries, London, JAC 006.

were still teeming with carp and, on one occasion, narrowly avoided being shot by Squire White for his trouble.

The modern appearance of both Kingtons embraces much 20th-century and newer residential development, attracted by easy access to Chippenham and the motorway. At Langley cul-de-sacs of houses have been built off Day's Lane, Church Road and Plough Lane during the 1980s and later, and there has been considerable infilling and redevelopment of older sites. The high street in Kington St Michael has also seen infilling and, at its northern end on both sides, limited housing development, in the form of closes and a primary school. A large warehousing and

Postcard showing the delights of Kington St Michael dated before 1952.

distribution centre was developed along the northern edge of Kington Langley parish after 2021 close to, and attracted by, the motorway junction.

Away from the modern villages, commerce and traffic, the Kingtons retain a landscape of scattered farmsteads linked by a network of lanes. The buildings are typically of stone derived from the locally quarried Cornbrash and Forest Marble limestones, 'fashioned out of the earth on which they stand', as Heather Tanner memorably described them. Most date from the 18th century or later, although Upper Swinley (1639) and Easton Piercy Manor Farm (1631) take us back to the world familiar to John Aubrey.

Case Study: Easton Piercy

EASTON PIERCY lies west of Kington St Michael. It is part of Kington St Michael parish, but it was not always so. Like Kington Langley, Easton was originally a separate settlement that became annexed to Kington. But unlike Kington Langley, Easton was not separated from Kington again.

The settlement, probably Saxon, appears to have been carved from the vast unenclosed area of common land that lay east of Yatton Keynell. Easton means the 'east farm' because it was east of Yatton. 'Piercy' was added to the name of the village from the family of Piers or Fitzpiers who occupied land here in the 13th century.

The medieval village consisted of Cromhall farm, named from the Anglo Saxon 'crooked corner', alongside, a manor house, a chapel, and a handful of cottages to the south-west of the manor. The village contracted in the mid-14th century after the plague devastated the local population. Between 1332 and 1377 the number of households appears to have been reduced by a third. The decline continued and the number of households

Easton Piercy, Manor House by Alfred Provis c.1845. Reproduced courtesy of Wiltshire Museum, Devizes, 1982.3140.

halved again between 1377 and 1662. Some cottages became abandoned as the land was given over to pasture. The transition of the agricultural focus from arable to dairy encouraged a movement away from a clustered village of cottages, manor, and chapel towards a dispersed settlement of farms.

Easton Piercy Manor House from the south sketched in 1851 and photographed in 1865. Reproduced courtesy of Society of Antiquaries, London, JAC 006.

View towards his childhood home at lower Easton Piercy by John Aubrey c.1669. Repro-
duced courtesy of the Bodleian Libraries, University of Oxford, MSS Aubrey 17, fol 10r.

   The original manor house was rebuilt by new owners c.1631 and
largely rebuilt again in the late 19th century. It is now called Manor Farm.
The chapel with graveyard (human remains were still found here during
the 19th century), stood to the north of the house. The chapel was
small but topped with a bell turret in which were mounted two small

a *thin blew landskape*

bells. It was pulled down seemingly at the same time as the new 17th-century manor was constructed, probably providing much of the stone. A stone cross stood by Cromhall Lane at the bend in the road beside the entrance to the manor. A 'font stone' served as a base into which the cross was fitted. The use of the cross is unknown, although it probably served as a place for preaching. Unfortunately, like the original manor and chapel, no representation of the cross remains, and it too, by c.1670, had been broken up. Its base was used at Cromhall for a water trough.

The Lyte family leased Easton Piercy from the 15th century and in 1574 purchased it in its entirety (save Cromhall), before dividing the estate up. Thereafter, the farms of Upper and Lower Easton Piercy were created.

John Aubrey, the 17th-century antiquary, was born at Lower Easton Piercy in 1626 and, in 1652 inherited it from his father who had married Deborah Lyte. Aubrey loved Easton Piercy but also craved the society of London and Oxford. Unsurprisingly, perhaps, he became dissatisfied with the homely Elizabethan pile of his childhood and began to design a home where he could entertain intellectual friends and study natural philosophy (nature and the physical universe), which was a life-long passion. In the design he was influenced by his cousin Sir John Danvers, 'who first taught us the ways of Italian gardens', and his estate at Lavington.

The house planned by John Aubrey at Easton Piercy, drawn c.1669. Reproduced courtesy of the Bodleian Libraries, University of Oxford, MSS Aubrey 17, fol 8r.

Aubrey's plans for a new house probably began in 1665 when he anticipated acquiring a fortune through marriage to Joane Sumner. His vision was for a neo-classical villa surrounded by an observatory, terraced gardens, grottos, water gardens and fountains, including one depicting Neptune (with a duck pursued by a spaniel). Like an artist, Aubrey planned the vistas from the house and gardens. But they were dreams never really

Aubrey's imagined Italianate views from the house he planned to build, including nuns walking through the gardens. Reproduced courtesy of the Bodleian Libraries, University of Oxford, MSS Aubrey 17, fol 15r.

likely to be translated into reality. They showed a house with no chimneys and highly problematic access to the front door or the lower levels of the garden. The views he sketched appeared more Italy than Wiltshire, replete with poplar trees and nuns walking the gardens. Nonetheless, the many sketches Aubrey made caused later writers on Kington, including John Britton and John Jackson, to be confused about whether they showed a plan or a real place.

Alas, his marriage never happened, and his affair ended in a costly lawsuit. And even as Aubrey made many of the sketches, he knew it was never to be and that he would give up the place 'which I so much love'. Yet, Easton remained at the centre of his writing after he sold the estate in 1670-1. Aubrey continued to style himself 'of Easton Piers', and even donated a specimen of the soil of his home to the Royal Society.

Unfortunately, by the 1780s the home of Aubrey's remembrance was in a state of ruin – covered in ivy, its doors and windows removed, and its floors decayed or fallen in. In one room were fragments of old armour. Subsequently 'a snug modern building' was erected on the spot.

Easton Piercy remains a small settlement comprising a collection of farms, just as rural as it was in Aubrey's time, although sadly without his beautiful, realised, vision.

Map of Kington St Michael parish including Kington Langley, made for John Britton in 1842. Reproduced courtesy of the Society of Antiquaries, London, JAC006.

PARISH OF KINGTON ST MICHAEL,

for Britton's History of KINGTON.

Linking the settlements, communal places and outlying farms, there had always been a network of local lanes, ways and paths, enabling parishioners to move livestock, attend church, take grain to the mill and travel to local markets. As Easton Piercy declined, its lines of communication atrophied – 'old ways now lost, but some vestigial left', as Aubrey described them. Not all disappeared, as some are recorded on 19th-century maps, and others, such as Cromhall Lane running west to Yatton Keynell, have survived as minor roads. An ancient trackway, described as such in 1518, led from Kington St Michael to Peckingell, and this presumably included the present road into the village from the traffic lights, and its opposite number in Kington Langley, Plough Lane. It would also have served as part of the route Kington Langley inhabitants would have taken when they needed to attend their parish church or the market at Kington St Michael. Aubrey speaks of a way running through Kington Langley, which probably included the present Church Road and the Common, then running across open country to Plough Lane and beyond. Many such minor roads are undatable, but there can be little doubt that Stanton Lane, running north from Kington St Michael to Swinley and beyond, and Day's Lane in Kington Langley, have been used for centuries.

The more significant routes through the parish served long-distance travellers as well as the local residents. Until the coming of the motorway in 1971 the most important of these were the roads running north from Chippenham towards Malmesbury and Swindon. The Malmesbury road may be named as a landmark, *Ergespath*, in the 940 Saxon charter; in 1653, by when road maintenance was a parish responsibility, its southern continuation to Chippenham was mapped as part of a remarkable agreement between officers of three parishes to share their highway responsibilities. The Swindon road, running past the eastern edge of Kington Langley common, was also part of this agreement, and was described as the highway commonly called Tedbury [Tetbury] or (confusingly) Malmesbury Way. Because of their importance, both came under the aegis of turnpike trusts in the 18th century, set up to improve roads from the proceeds of tolls charged on travellers. The present Malmesbury road was turnpiked in 1756 and remained a toll road until about 1868. In 1922 it was classified as an A road, A429, but renumbered A350 when it was reconstructed as a dual

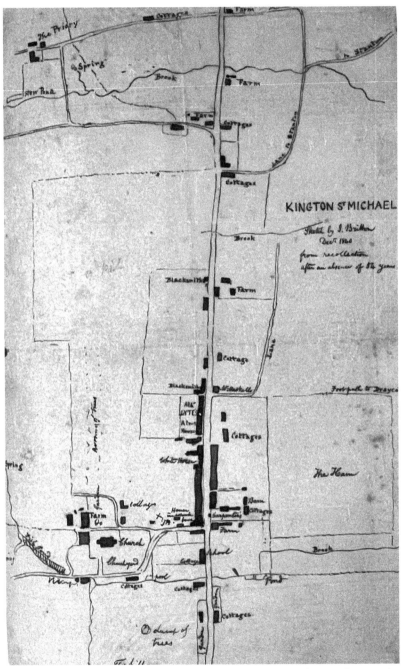

*Map of Kington St Michael drawn by John Britton in 1840 after an absence of 54
years. Reproduced courtesy of Wiltshire Museum, Devizes, M286.*

carriageway to feed the motorway junction which opened in 1971. The Swindon road had been turnpiked earlier, in 1727, as far as Draycot Cerne. It too became an A road (A420) in the 1920s, but was demoted when the motorway opened and traffic decreased.

Away from the turnpikes, the parish roads were in poor condition until the 19th century. According to John Britton, before 1800 they, 'were not easy to be passed over by carriages; for being only used by waggons and carts, they were worn into two deep ruts by the wheels, and another nearly equally deep by the horses'. No railways pass through the parish, and no Victorian country carriers are recorded as based in the Kingtons. The villages were probably served by carriers journeying weekly to Chippenham from places further north. Only in 1922 were they served by motorised public transport, when buses between Malmesbury and Chippenham began to operate, with improvements to the service in 1929 and later.

When the 19th century began the combined population of the Kingtons was 729, of which around half lived in Kington Langley. Two hundred years on the total has doubled and stabilised, at around 800 in Kington Langley and 700 in Kington St Michael and Easton Piercy. In between there have been fluctuations. A high point of 1,219, roughly equally divided between the two communities, was achieved in the 1850s, but then they experienced a decline – in common with rural Wiltshire generally – to a little over 400 in each by 1900. New housing development from the 1950s onwards has boosted the population, which is probably greater now than at any point in the Kington's history.

Estimating population before 1800 is challenging. Domesday book records 24 households on the Glastonbury estate in 1086, which had risen to 56 by 1189. The Black Death of 1348-9 appears to have struck a terrible blow, perhaps reducing the population at a stroke to less than half, from which the community struggled to recover. In 1377, when a poll tax was levied on all adults, 93 paid in Kington St Michael and 111 in Kington Langley. No reliable statistic is available after that until 1676, when the adult population of the Kingtons combined was recorded as 361. This would perhaps represent a total of about 580 if children were included, so a significant increase in population occurred during the later 17th century and through the 18th, to arrive at 729 by 1800.

Such a rise is reflected perhaps in the survival of a number of examples of cottages of rubblestone under slate or tile roofs which date from this period, and of several more substantial farmhouses. Cared-for, improved and protected now, they do not represent the spartan living conditions that John Britton remembers as a child in the 1780s. He grew up in one of the many such cottages that have since fallen down. They were of the humblest and poorest kind, he recalled, 'with walls of rough undressed stone and mortar, thatched roofs, stone slabs from the quarries, or the bare earth for the floor, windows of varied forms and sizes, many of them papered or boarded, or with broken glass'. Britton, a sophisticated architectural historian, was probably excessively harsh on the housing stock of his native parish. A number of notable high-status buildings have survived, including the parish church, the prioress' lodgings, and the fine row of almshouses at Kington St Michael which we shall encounter in later chapters.

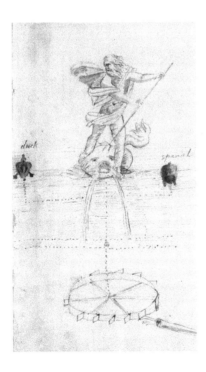

Diorama of a medieval village showing ploughing. The scene shows the system of strip farming where the land was laid out in large open fields and then distributed between villagers in the form of long strips. Source: Science Museum Group. Creative Commons licence. Attribution 4.0 International (CC by 4.0).

2
CULTIVATION, COMMERCE AND CONTAMINATION

THE ANGLO-SAXON ESTATES of Kington St Michael with Kington Langley provided food and revenues for the King's residence at Chippenham. The Crown had granted most of the lands to Glastonbury abbey by 1066 and instead they provided produce and revenues to the abbey until the reformation in the 16th century.

In 1189 an abbey survey was conducted, which provides a snapshot of how the estate was organised under the feudal system and who lived in the villages. Cultivated and fallow land, woods, and pasture surrounded the villages. The tenants, or villeins, were technically the property of the abbot as lord of the manor. Some, like Dunwine, Guarin, Helyas and Sewine, were known only by their Christian names. Others had names which alluded to their colouring or a second occupation aside from that of a farmer, such as William the Blond and Robert the Smith. In addition to paying a fee to the abbey for their holdings, the villeins had to perform services for the lord. These usually involved working on the demesne, but three men – the abbot's bailiff Roger, William of Perrier and Osbert White – were also obliged to take three cartloads of goods to Bristol, from where the loads were probably taken on to Glastonbury abbey or sold at market.

Helyas held half a hide, approximately 60 acres,

for six shillings and should do other customary services. If the lord wishes, the tenant must give three shillings and work for two days a week and plough half an acre every Friday between the feast of St. Michael (29 September) and the feast of St. Martin (11 November). Between the feast of St. Martin and Hockday (the week after Easter), he should plough a quarter of an acre on Fridays. And from Hockday to the birth of St. John (24 June), he should hoe half an acre every Friday. And if he does the work, then they shall give two sheaves of wheat.

Obligations varied according to the size of the holding. Dunwine who had a large holding was obliged to mow and cart hay and to plough three times. In contrast, Sibil, a single woman with a cottage, a croft (probably an enclosed garden for vegetable cultivation) and one acre of land, was obliged to mow two acres and gather the hay. She had to work every day through the harvest when her meal was provided by the lord, otherwise she was only expected to work on a Monday. Duties provided included weeding, ploughing, mowing and stacking hay. Arable cultivation took place in three large fields. Tenants had strips, which they were expected to keep drained and ditched; their plots probably had boundary markers known as merestones. The farming was mixed, and aside from arable on the demesne there were cattle, sheep and pigs.

The parish priest, John, had a cottage and garden and one virgate, or approximately 30 acres of land. He was not required to provide any further service. Another virgate was provided for the maintenance of the

Above: Peasants harvesting wheat while others relax. The Harvesters Pieter Breughel the Elder 1565. Public Domain
Previous pages: View from 'upper sheep house meade', a position possibly slightly south west of Tor Hill (between West Lodge and Down Farm), showing a sheep field, enclosed by woods and orchard with the steeple of Kington St Michael beyond by John Aubrey c.1669. Source: Bodleian Libraries, University of Oxford, MSS Aubrey 17, fol 6r.

chapel at Langley. Several hundred acres were held in common and used for communal grazing and wood-gathering. Separate from this was an additional 40 acres of common land for tenants at Kington Langley.

The estate also had a mill, probably Byde mill in the north of Kington Langley, for grinding the grain grown locally. It was tenanted by Peter de Estune. At the time of the survey, Peter was in dispute with the estate, arguing that given the money he paid, he was entitled to have a road (*via*) to the mill.

Aside from the tenants of the estate there were three freeholders who held land directly from the Crown. They included Robert Courtney, son-in-law of Reginald Fitzurse, who had been one of the archbishop's murderers in 1170. Robert held the Fitzurse estate, a holding of approximately 240 acres. He was likely non-resident in Langley as he had his own bailiff, Garwi, who administered the Fitzurse estate. Robert, may have been unpopular as Garwi had taken land from one of the Glastonbury abbey tenants by force. If the abbey sought to recover their property from Robert and Garwi it is not recorded.

A weekly Tuesday market and an annual three-day fair were granted to Kington St Michael in 1266. Tolls paid by stall holders for the fair in 1335 raised £1 4s. 6d. but by 1564 £1 6s. 8d. was still being paid, suggesting that in the intervening 200 years the fair had not been developed. However, it was still enjoyed a hundred years later during the lifetime of John Aubrey in the 17th century, who described it as famous for ale and geese. Meanwhile, the weekly market had changed too. No longer held on a Tuesday, Aubrey described it as a 'little' market held on Friday 'for fish, eggs, butter, and such small gear'; and he suggested that by the reformation it had been chiefly held for the nuns of St Mary's priory. The market and fair were held at the cross, which may have stood on or near the recreation ground between Grove Lane and Honey Knob Hill.

Part of the park of the manor of Kington St Michael sketched by John Aubrey c.1670 possibly showing the parsonage as it then existed. Reproduced courtesy of the Bodleian Libraries, University of Oxford, MSS Aubrey 3, fol 62r

The people of Tournai bury victims of the Black Death. Miniature by Pierart dou Tielt. Public Domain via Wikimedia commons

Case Study: Plague and Pestilence

THE BLACK DEATH arrived in England at Weymouth, Dorset, sometime in May or June 1348. It quickly spread through the surrounding countryside and along principal routes out of the town. The contagion had reached Wiltshire by August and radiated quickly from population centres into the countryside, probably hitting Kington St. Michael over the winter of 1348-9. Perhaps it came from a traveller or trader who brought rat fleas with their merchandise into the village. St Mary's priory would have been a considerable local draw. However it was brought, it certainly did arrive; by Easter 1349, 56% of the landless men and boys named and counted for tax purposes at Easter the previous year were dead. These were predominantly young, fit men, and the effects of the plague were likely to have impacted on the rest of the population just as much. The nuns at the priory and local churchmen may have been particularly affected as many residents would have turned to them for medical and spiritual help. It is doubtless no coincidence that in 1349 a new prioress, Lucy Paas, was elected, and a new vicar, Richard Thomelyn, was appointed.

The symptoms of the plague were all too apparent. Firstly, the appearance of painful bubos (swollen lymph nodes) in the groin, neck and armpits, which later secreted pus and blood. It was followed by acute fever and vomiting blood. Victims usually died between two and seven days after the initial infection, and the death rate was probably a terrifying 60 to 90 per cent. Medical assistance probably involved bloodletting, vomiting and sweating, but such care was futile and the disease ravaged the rich and poor alike. The dead of Kington included John Snel, Henry Monjoye, Gilbert Beneyt, Miles le Hoppere, William Nichole, and John Palling. Their names were recorded centuries before the parish registers were created because of a local head tax collected from landless males over the age of 13. Tens or even hundreds more men, women and children also died, but their names are lost to history. Village tradition suggests that plague victims were buried, perhaps these named men among them, in an area to the south of the chancel.

Besides the unimaginable personal crises, this massive fall in the population significantly changed the parish economy. Local agriculture relied on a large pool of labourers to sow, weed and harvest crops, but these workers were gone almost overnight. There was no immediate recovery, and for the next fifty years, at least, the population continued to decline. The community needed more men to be able to grow crops in the heavy, waterlogged soils. Consequently, only the best soils were still planted with crops, and a transition to less labour-intensive livestock farming became inevitable. For those households who remained, the change probably resulted in an improved diet containing more high-quality proteins and fewer lean years when there was barely enough to eat.

With the change in the number or people available to work the land traditional tenant and landlord relationships began to break down after the plague. Gradually the villeins in Kington St Michael and Kington Langley paid fines for their personal freedom (manumission), and there was a transition from villein to copyhold tenure in the 14th and 15th centuries. However, as late as 1562 a resident, Nicholas Russell, who had been born into bondage, paid for his manumission, his release from being bound to the lord and the manor.

As devastating as it was in the 14th century, it was by no means the only occurrence of the plague. In 1582, the arrival and departure of the plague were marked in the parish registers on 4 May and 6 August, respectively. Of the 18 deaths recorded in that outbreak, eight were from one family. According to a village tradition recorded by Francis Kilvert in his diary, Kington was 'green with grass during the *Great Plague* for there was scarcely any passing in those dreadful months.'

The Snells' mansion house at Kington St Michael sketched by John Aubrey c.1670 built on the site of the former abbey grange. Reproduced courtesy of the Bodleian Libraries, University of Oxford, MSS Aubrey 3, fol 62r.

At the dissolution of the monasteries the former estate of Glastonbury abbey at Kington St Michael and Kington Langley passed to Nicholas Snell, whose father had been the abbot's reeve. This estate, thereafter, was inherited by his son, John, and grandson Charles. Charles was known by John Aubrey who observed that he was 'an honest young gent but kept a perpetual sott [a fool]' by Sir Walter Raleigh who persuaded him to build a ship called the *Angel Gabriel*. Building the ship cost Snell his manor at Yatton Keynell, the farm at Easton Piercy, Thornhill and more. The ship was then forfeited by Raleigh when he was tried for treason. A sott Charles may have been, but under his father and grandfather farming in the villages changed. In 1518 the community enjoyed the use of *c.* 400 acres at Heywood at Kington St Michael as communal pasture. Fifty years later the wood had been reduced to 200 acres, and Heywood was then enclosed to be almost entirely reserved for the private use of the Snell estate. The park that ran south from the Snell's manor house adjacent to St Michael's church at Kington and grounds that ran north to the present Ridings were also lost to the community. Meanwhile, an expanse of common land called Langley Heath was likewise almost entirely enclosed. Open fields communally cultivated for centuries became enclosed during the mid-17th century. As a consequence of these changes John Aubrey noted that Snell's tenants 'live poorly and needily'. However, local people had not suffered in silence; they had resisted the encroachment of their traditional rights for several decades by repeatedly taking wood and pasturing animals in areas where they had formerly held rights to do so.

Farms required allied trades and there is evidence of blacksmiths, carpenters and masons from at least the 17th century. However, despite the presence of the weekly market and annual fair, Kington St Michael with Kington Langley had very little by way of medieval retail, although two alehouse keepers were fined in 1418. Later, during the 1560s and 1570s the manor court regularly recorded three brewers, who often acted as alehouse keepers, and one or two bakers. A Walter Williams leased a property called 'the Killing House' in 1564, probably the village slaughterhouse. A butcher by the name of Richard Welsted moved from Kington St Michael to trade instead in Kington Langley in 1574. Two years later, Kington Langley had both a butcher and baker. In the late 16th century, the Kingtons also had their own 'merchant', Richard Powre, a purveyor of a range of goods Unfortunately, Richard was not the most ethical of retailers and was regularly fined for selling goods at excessive prices.

Textiles

John Britton was born in the parish of Kington St Michael with Kington Langley in 1771. In his autobiography, written towards the end of his life, Britton confidently declared, 'there has never, in fact, been a loom in this parish.' He was wrong. In 1189, 'William the weaver' was amongst the tenants of Glastonbury abbey on their estate in Kington. Later, there is evidence that woollen cloth manufacture took place across the parish, although predominantly

Woman Spinning by Jacques Adrien Lavieille after Jean-François Millet. Public Domain via Wikipedia Commons.

in Kington Langley, throughout the 17th and 18th centuries, and was undertaken at four properties in Kington Langley as late as 1833.

During the 17th and 18th centuries the production of woollen cloth was organised by local clothiers who employed workers to spin the wool into yarn and weave the yarn into cloth. Women were primarily involved in spinning, while men took the more lucrative job of weaving. Both occupations could occur within the same household, but the wives of local agricultural labourers also undertook spinning to generate an additional income. Weaving was a skilled occupation that took place domestically but in a 'shop' (meaning workshop). Looms were valuable. Although weaving was largely done by men, there were exceptions. Mary Swayne at Byde Mill owned a loom on her death, which she left to her son, Thomas, in 1621.

Both broad and narrow cloth were woven locally. Broadcloth was woven up to 75% wider than its finished width. It was then taken to a fulling mill outside the parish, probably in Chippenham, to be shrunk and thickened. Several weavers wove serge cloth, a heavy material probably used for tailored items such as greatcoats or suits. Some weavers were well off. Serge weaver, Thomas Godwin, left an estate in 1735 that ran into hundreds of pounds. He left his home to his son but also £50 to each of his granddaughters and one guinea to a servant. Others were not so fortunate as Thomas Godwin; a century before, the weaver John Hodson had been so poor that his clothing was sold to pay for his funeral expenses.

Several local weavers had their possessions itemised in a probate inventory after they passed away, offering us some insight into how they lived. Thomas Tanner of Kington Langley, for instance, died in 1671. He was a weaver and probably a widower. He was seemingly an educated man, as he owned two bibles and a collection of other books. On the ground floor of his home was a hall and a buttery with a small room off it. The hall was the main living space and had a table with benches, three chairs, a few shelves, and a cupboard. The focus of the room was undoubtedly the large fireplace where meals were cooked. The utensils in the small chamber and buttery, with collections of tubs, barrels, brass pots, pans and knives, pewter tankards, dishes, candlesticks and frying pan, plus a butter churn and cheese press, suggest that this was where the household's food was prepared. Upstairs were two bedrooms and a

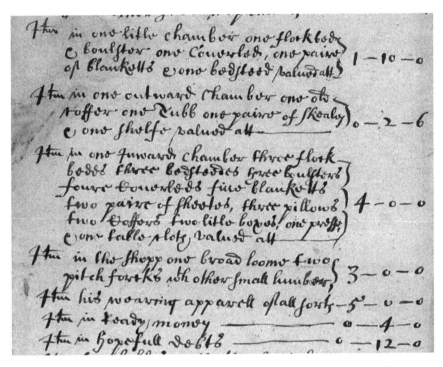

Part of the inventory of the goods of Thomas Tanner weaver of Kington Langley 1671. Reproduced courtesy of Salisbury Diocese and the Wiltshire and Swindon History Centre, Chippenham, P1/T/161.

storeroom. In the first bedroom, the 'little' chamber, was one bed and no other furniture, the mattress was flock, made of wool refuse. In the second sleeping chamber were three beds likewise made of flock. Only two of the four beds had sheets. The beds may have slept several people, including Thomas's grown-up children. Separately listed was Thomas's weaving shop, where he had his broadloom. Outside was a cow house, orchard, garden and ten acres of land. He left his home to his son, also called Thomas, but he also bequeathed property and money to his other children. Thomas's sibling, David was left their father's broadloom.

As Thomas's inventory suggests, it was common for those in the cloth trade to grow produce and keep livestock for household consumption. For some individuals, farming was a substantial concern. When serge maker William Brite died in 1722, he had a 17-strong dairy herd, as well as calves and young heifers. He also had two pigs, a horse, and a fully equipped dairy, which produced cheese (a widespread domestic industry in this part of Wiltshire) and further utensils that suggested he was brewing beer. A little later, John Britton's father was a shopkeeper, maltster, small farmer and baker.

Commerce

Throughout the 17th and 18th centuries the villages of Kington St Michael and Kington Langley continued to have limited commerce apart from what was necessary to meet the essential requirements of the community. It was quite common for those engaged in commerce, like John Britton's father, to have more than one occupation, and this may have been supported by keeping livestock and growing produce. In 1867 the craftsmen and retailers that serviced the needs of Kington St Michael included Amelia Barnes, a baker and maltster; David Rumming, a baker and farmer; Maria Granger, a beer seller; Thomas Sealy, a blacksmith and carpenter; Henry Smith, another blacksmith; Joseph Dyer, a carpenter and wheelwright; George Gainey, a shopkeeper and butcher; John Jones, William Whittle and George Wiltshire, who were all shopkeepers; John Sealy, a tailor and, finally, William Compton the village thatcher. Meanwhile at Kington Langley trade was dominated by Jeremiah Ashe a shopkeeper and the local Baptist minister; Lewin Hadrill and

PARNELL & SON

(LIONEL A. G. PARNELL)

BAKERS, GROCERS,
and GENERAL
PROVISION MERCHANTS.

LANGLEY FITZURSE.

Established 1850   Gold Medal and other Awards
Tel. Kington Langley 246.

Advert for Parnell and Son, Kington Langley from 1960.

Arthur Parnell, beer sellers; George May and Jesse Cole both farmers and butchers; and Saul Cole a baker and maltster. George Little was sub-postmaster in 1895 when the Langley community also enjoyed the services of a grocer, beer retailer, shopkeeper, blacksmith, wheelwright, mason and three carpenters.

Women and work

There were seemingly few opportunities for women during the medieval and early modern period to attain roles of economic importance. Nonetheless, despite obstacles, such as surrendering the right to hold and control property on marriage, some of the women of the Kingtons, outside the priory of St Mary's which is discussed separately, held estates, ran businesses or were in paid employment.

In 1189, over 10% of the holders of property on the Kington St Michael and Kington Langley manor of the abbey of Glastonbury were women. Adel, widow of Robert de Abbedestona (Abson), was a freeholder who held approximately 240 acres, almost one quarter of the entire acreage of the manor. The widow Elviva was one of the most significant tenants. Other female tenants were Adel, Sibil and Edeta. Emma de Meisi held 25 acres of land which appears to have been carved from the manor's common land. The annotation in the survey suggests that the death of abbot Robert had allowed Emma to make this illicit encroachment. As Emma still held the land 15 years after the abbot's demise it is likely that she had managed to retain the land by paying for a retrospective enclosure licence.

One of the most fascinating influences of women at Kington St Michael with Kington Langley was the role played by them in the descent of Glastonbury abbey's manor. After the reformation the manor had descended through the Snell family until the death of Charles Snell in 1651. The ownership of the manor was then divided between his sister Mary Gastrell and the heirs of his two deceased sisters Penelope Newman and Barbara Stokes. A manor divided in three was not too difficult to administer, but in the next generation Penelope Newman's share was divided between her three daughters and a generation later Mary Gastrell's share was divided between her five daughters. It soon became impossible to reconcile these competing interests and the manor broke up.

When a daughter inherited a share of a manor it might be administered by her husband on her behalf, and this might also be true

of manorial tenants who held lands by copy of court roll. At Kington
St Michael in 1655 Samuel Tanner, Richard Hine and John Plant all
held their lands through their wife's inheritance. The widows had more
control and are named in their own right as property holders: Jane Aland
held a house, garden and 32 acres of land, Anne Tanner had a house
and 22 acres, Alice Tanner had a house and 14 acres. In all nine of the
58 tenants at Kington St Michael and Kington Langley in 1655 were
widows. These women had a significant impact on the village economy,
Jane Aland, Anne Tanner and Alice Tanner had control over some of the
more valuable properties in their village. Later in the century another
widow, Mary White, ran a mixed arable and dairy farm at Easton Piercy.
At her death her estate was worth over £100.

Women could also have paid occupations or businesses. One of the
most enigmatic was Elizabeth Tayler who died in 1593. Elizabeth plied
the trade of 'fortune teller'. Another fascinating woman was the alehouse
keeper, Edith Brown.

*Entertaining at an alehouse door. Etching by J. Taylor (?), c. 1800, after G. Tilborgh
1625– c.1678. Source: Wellcome Collection.*

Case Study: Edith Brown

O NE OF THE FEW TRADES in which medieval and early modern women
could participate independently of men was brewing and selling
alcohol. Edith was involved in this trade by 1562, if not before. Given her
longevity, it was one she was good at. Edith ran an alehouse from her
cottage where locals gathered to socialise, drink, and eat. She also sold
alcohol for consumption at home and it is possible that she sometimes
let weary travellers stay the night. Establishments like hers in Kington
(there were one or maybe two others) provided one of the few places of
recreation and social life apart from St Michael's church.

When Edith was open for business she likely displayed an 'ale-stick'
outside, traditionally a stick with a brush at one end. This has led some
historians to suggest women employed in brewing were associated in
the popular imagination with witches. Inside the alehouses of the period,
drinkers sat on benches and stools against trestle tables. A fire was an
important aspect and provided the focal point in the drinking areas. The
house is likely to have been filled to capacity during Kington's Tuesday
market or over the three-day Michaelmas fair.

As with many publicans today, the alehouse was also Edith's home.
The wider Browne family were largely tenant farmers of the estate of the
Snell family. Edith's husband, John, held little parcels of land to the west of
the main village street and south west of the village next to Heywood. It
was probably on one of these that their cottage-cum-alehouse stood.

At the outset, Edith worked alongside John. In 1562 she was
censured by the manor court for allowing drinking past the hour of 9 pm
in the evening. As the authorities chose to condemn Edith herself, it is
probable that she was the principal partner in the business. In 1568 John
stopped his involvement. As he died the following year, it is likely that in
1568 his health was already failing.

The alehouse was now Edith's own. She did not remarry. Any
new husband would have acquired all her property, a circumstance of
which she would have been aware. Instead Edith chose to keep her
independence, and, likely assisted by her unmarried daughters, Agnes and
Joan, she continued trading for a number of years.

Edith was not the only female alehouse keeper in Kington, another
was Margery Russell. Unlike Edith, Margery was censured many times

over the years. Like Edith, she had allowed drinking after 9 pm in 1562, but over the years she had also permitted 'illicit games' and 'gaming', sold illegal measures of alcohol and had not offered her customers victuals. Her house was once out of repair and several times Margery had committed trespass, probably by allowing her livestock to stray onto someone else's land . Edith kept to the rules of their trade and Margery did not.

In agricultural communities like Kington, people depended on their own good health and local agriculture for their livelihoods. One bad harvest and people quickly became malnourished. Two, and there was a real chance of starvation. Communities were vigilant for signs of looming disaster, of portents and signs. When things went wrong during this period, individuals and sometimes whole communities would place the blame on the evil eye, fairies, witchcraft, or some other devilry. This may have been the case in 1574, when Edith was accused of witchcraft alongside her daughters, Joan and Agnes. According to a charge made at the Kington manorial court leet (where minor crimes and misdemeanours were dealt with within the community), the women were leading suspicious lives and were suspected of witchcraft. We do not know who first made the accusation, and what evidence was presented to the court, but it may have been no coincidence that in 1574, a Stephen Browne, presumably a relative of Edith's husband, first set himself up as a local brewer. Maybe the accusation was founded on familial spite or jealousy. Either way, the report does not appear to have been taken too seriously, or perhaps she was able to disprove it, as Edith and her daughters were not handed to the civil authorities, and she continued to ply her trade. In 1564 Agnes Mylles, a widow at nearby Stanley, had been accused of witchcraft and handed to local justices. She had been tried and hanged for witchcraft. Meanwhile, Edith was more fortunate and continued to work as a brewer until at least 1577, after which the manorial records are lost. It is pertinent that by then, Stephen Browne was no longer trading as a brewer.

Edith lived until December 1591 when her burial was recorded in registers at St Michael's, Kington St Michael. She had run a successful business as a widow in Elizabethan England for more than 20 years, no mean feat. She had also faced censure and an accusation which could have ended her life. Edith Brown was a remarkable woman.

There were ways in which women could try to safeguard or
perpetuate property being held by other women. For example, the
women of Kington St Michael in possession of property and businesses
sometimes left estates to other women to the virtual exclusion of
men in their families. When Elizabeth Tanner of Kington St Michael
died in 1696 she left son William one shilling, but all her estate to her
unmarried daughter Elizabeth, who was also her sole executrix. In 1705
another woman, the unmarried Latimer Tanner, left all her 'lands,
messuages [houses] and tenements' to her unmarried sister, Anne, 'to be
possessed and enjoyed'. While Anne enjoyed the estate Latimer gave her,
Latimer left their brother 2s. 6d.

Possibly one of the most successful early modern business owners
was Katherine Smith. A Quaker, Katherine was a widow who ran a shop
during the early 18th century. Unfortunately, although her stock was
valuable and stored in lockable boxes, it was not itemised by appraisers
of her probate inventory at her death in 1712, so we do not know the
precise nature of her business. She allowed her customers to run a line of
credit, and at her death the debt to her business alone was valued at £50.
Katherine also favoured her female family, leaving unmarried daughter
Elizabeth her entire business and making her sole executrix. Her son
William, meanwhile, was given her second best bed.

The presence in many probate inventories of the utensils of
cheese making indicates the local importance of cheese making to local
farming. According to
John Aubrey in the 17th
century the local profusion
of 'sower' plants helped
to create quality cheese.
Traditionally cheese
making was the preserve
of women, usually either
the farmer's wife or under
her direct management.

Illustration of a cheese press,
by Robin Tanner. Wiltshire Life
Society Collection. Reproduced
courtesy of Wiltshire Museum,
AVBGB.GBP399.

The widow, Edith Hawkins of Kington Langley had several cows and one pig on her death in 1605 and may have been supporting herself by cheese making and brewing given items in her probate inventory. Mary Swayne possessed a loom at her death in 1621 but was also cheese making. Women continued to be the local producers of cheese into the 19th century and until the last quarter of the century cheese making was centred on farm production.

In 1840 women controlled many of the farms in the Kingtons, not merely the means of dairy production. Mary Gaby jointly owned the Manor farm at Kington St Michael, along with other land and property extending to 298 acres. Betty Cole owned and ran a farm at Kington Langley and leased out other property. Other women landowners included Eliza Gabriel, Catherine Gale, Mary Mailard, Mary and Elizabeth Smith. Women were not just farmers and landowners. In 1848 Hannah Tucker was running the only shop listed in *Kelly's Wiltshire Directory* for Kington St Michael. She was still trading ten years later, by which time Maria Lane had started up as a shopkeeper in Kington Langley. Also at Kington Langley, Soloma Clark was described as a schoolmistress over a decade before the village school was built.

As the 19th century continued women became more visible in the workplace, often in positions connected with domestic service, education, or nursing. According to the 1911 census working women in Kington St Michael included Rhoda Pearce, who was a dressmaker, Susannah Sealy a milliner, Mabel Last the head teacher at the school, and Ellen Wittingham a laundress. Elizabeth Keynes was helping to run the bakery and Mary Anne Hulbert was caretaker at the reading room (a small local library). However, there were other women whose working contribution was invisible. Mary Gainey, whose husband was a carter, kept house and looked after the couple's seven children 13 years and under, a significant feat in a small cottage. At the White Horse Inn, Thomas Aland was listed as a brewer, and although his wife, Mary Ann, had no trade listed on the form it is almost inconceivable that she was not at work serving behind the bar, as did Elizabeth Martin at the White Hart Inn. Elizabeth also had seven children at home.

Later Agriculture

Between the 17th and 19th centuries the balance of agricultural land in Kington Langley shifted from arable to pasture, especially with the development of dairy herds. As the number of cows increased, sheep numbers declined, and by 1920 no sheep were kept on local farms. In 1943 there were still 17 farms in Kington Langley. The largest, Southsea farm with 432 acres was leased from Lord Glentoran and Trinity College Cambridge. Langley Gate farm had 206 acres and was owned and occupied by W L Collins. The wartime Ministry of Food noted a need to modernise farm buildings and poor drainage in farms across the parish.

Southsea Farm, Kington Langley photographed at the time of its sale in 1920 with (overleaf) description from the sale catalogue. Reproduced courtesy of Wiltshire and Swindon History Centre, 1043/6.

Some farmers were subject to particular criticism. Aside from only 'fair' drainage, the Limes farm was infested with moles and wireworms, heavily weeded, and its fencing and ditches were in poor condition. The Ministry of Food noted that food production was consequently 'LOW'. Kington St Michael observed similar trends with shifts to pasture, and problems with drainage and outdated buildings and farming methods. By

COLOURED PINK ON PLAN—No. 1.

Excellent Dairy and Mixed Farm

Situate in the Parishes of KINGTON LANGLEY and DRAYCOT, with good approach and long frontages to the Main Road, known as

"SOUTHSEA FARM"

WITH

—— EXCELLENT WATER SUPPLY. ——

The Residential Farmhouse

Looks out upon the

LAWNS and ORCHARD,

Is well planned, and contains Hall, Breakfast-room, Dining-room, Office, Kitchen (H. & C.), Dairy and other Offices, Five Bedrooms, Two Attics and Bath-room, Boot and Wood-houses, Engine-house,

ORCHARD AND KITCHEN GARDEN.

Extensive Modern well-arranged OUTBUILDINGS

Include Milk-house, Nag and Hunter Stabling, Trap-house and Harness-room, Three Pigstyes, Three-bay Shed, Large Implement Shed, Lean-to Shed, Barn, Stable, Two Calf-houses, Chaff and Root-house, Six-tie Cart-horse Stable,

TIE-UP ACCOMMODATION FOR FORTY-FIVE COWS,

Cattle Sheds, Hay-houses, etc.

First-class Six-bay CORN BARN and Five-bay DUTCH HAY BARN.

In Field No. 27 is a well-built Three-bay Cattle Shed with yard and galvanised Lean-to, which together with the

Healthy Pasture and Easy-working Arable

CONTAIN A TOTAL AREA OF

226a   3r   10p

21

the time of the Second World War the two largest farms, Yatton Manor farm, 276 a., and Allington Manor farm, 309 a., were based outside the parish. Others were too small to remain independently viable by the mid-20th century, and across the two parishes landholdings were consolidated. Agriculture was no longer the biggest employer and by 1955 it was noted that most Kington Langley people were employed outside the parish.

An Indignant Husband by Thomas Rowlandson.
Source: Royal Collection.

3.
MISDEEDS, MANORS & MANAGEMENT

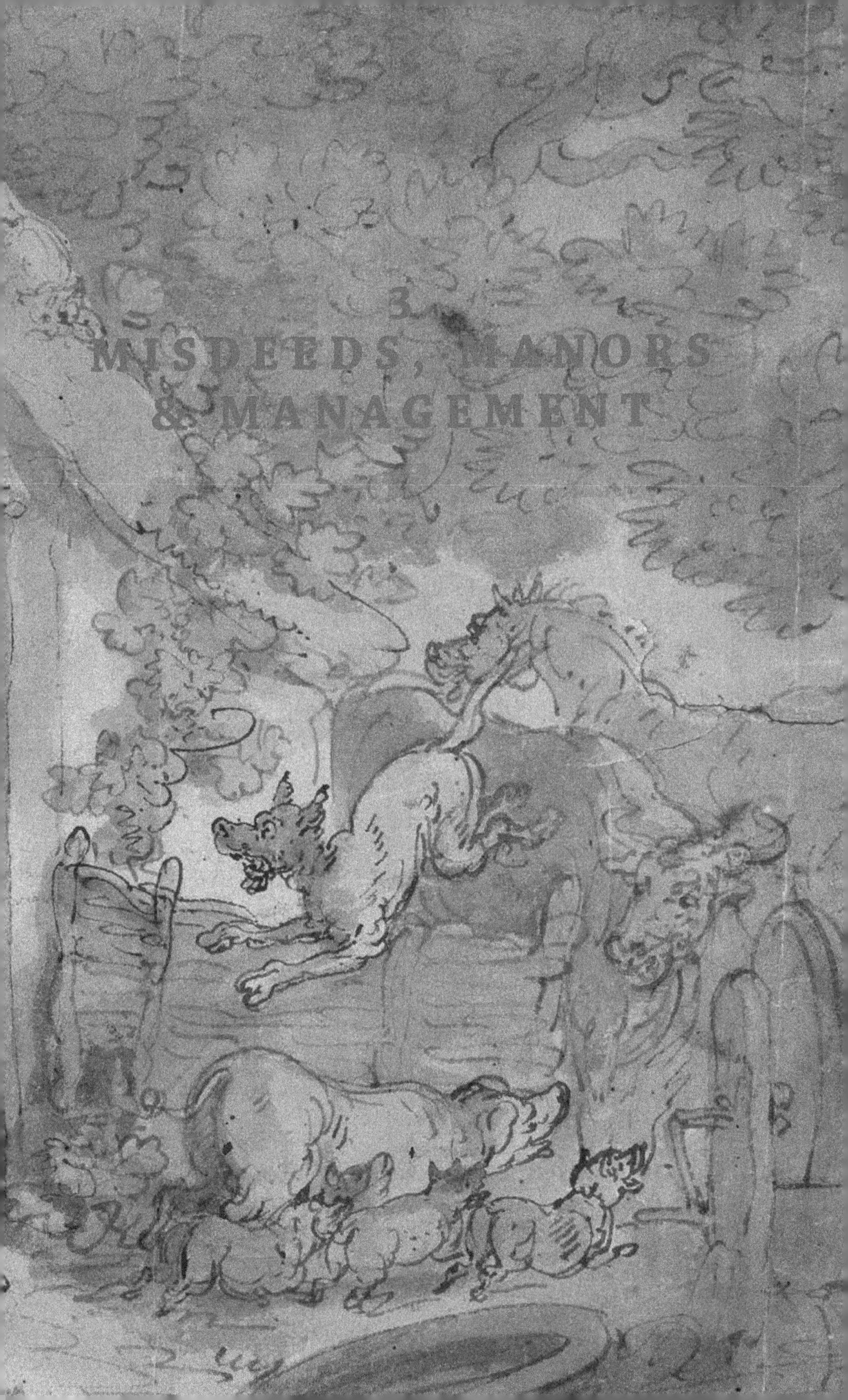

ONE OF THE FIRST CRIMES recorded for Kington St Michael and Kington Langley was in the 1230s when John Oliver accused Henry Crock of robbery and assault. A decade later, Edith, daughter of Richard le Munner and Alice de Firmar, was murdered near St. Mary's Priory. The case was dealt with in 1249. Unfortunately no prosecution followed, and presumably there was no justice for Edith. Seventy years later, there was yet another homicide, but in this case, there was a prosecution.

The events took place in October 1304. Miles de Ciston was at Sarah Fitzurse's home, most likely Fitzurse manor at Kington Langley. The nature of their relationship was not stated in court proceedings, but Robert de Middelhop, who probably lived locally, was riven with jealousy to such an extent that he came to the house intending to slay Miles. Robert broke the chamber door where Miles (and presumably Sarah) were together. Robert's sword was drawn, and he struck Miles twice. Miles ran for his life but was pursued into a corner. His back to the wall, Miles then drew a dagger and stabbed Robert in the heart killing him. It appeared at the trial to be a case of self-defence. A few months later Miles was 'remanded for grace' to await the King's pardon for slaying Robert. But the story was more complex. The court also recorded that Miles had killed Robert's brother. Although no details are given, Miles was likewise remanded for grace for that crime. Maybe the second death made the self-defence argument problematical because, subsequently, Miles was not pardoned as expected, but instead hanged for murder.

Fortunately, most offences recorded for the villages were not of such an extreme nature, and many were dealt with in the parish. The medieval manor court of Kington St Michael and Kington Langley met twice a year at Kington St Michael and was responsible for resolving minor misdemeanours. While much business concerned stray animals or those who neglected to repair boundaries, fences and highways or scour their ditches, public order offences were sometimes dealt with too. The court was presided over by a bailiff and steward from Glastonbury abbey, which owned most of the land and property in Kington St Michael and Kington Langley.

During the reformation in the mid-16th century Glastonbury abbey and St Mary's priory at Kington St Michael were dissolved. Their estates passed into the hands of private owners, but the manor court continued to be held. The court business was recorded in the manor court book. This survives from 1558; surprisingly, the volume is wrapped in a 14th-century manuscript, a commentary on the Epistle of Hebrews from the New Testament, which may have survived the dissolution of the priory.

Part of a 14th-century manuscript that wraps the manor court book for Kington St Michael. Reproduced courtesy of Salisbury Diocese and the Wiltshire and Swindon History Centre, C/C/Bish/459/1.

Stocks being used as a punishment for minor misdemeanours. Coloured etching by Thomas Rowlandson. 8 March 1790. Source the Royal Collection.

Under the local organisation of the manorial system, separate 'tithingmen' were selected for Kington St Michael and Kington Langley. The tithingman was a petty constable or law enforcement officer. The position was unpaid but probably not more demanding than requiring the presentation of small misdemeanours to the manor court. These misdeeds included fist fights, illicit ball games, the excessive charges of local millers and, in 1576, the case of John Dyke, who permitted games in his house and set a bad example to all his neighbours. Miscreants were often charged fines. In 1564 at Kington Langley, Richard Cooke sought the highest damages possible at the court (39s. 10d.) in a complaint against Robert Taylor because 'that thy wife haste hurt my child and also my cattell by thy cursing.' However, there were also local stocks in

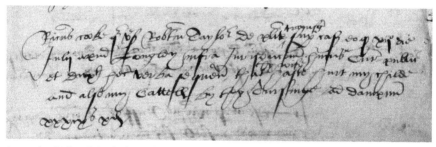

A case by Richard Cooke brought against Robert Taylor in 1564 following Robert's wife's cursing. Reproduced courtesy of Salisbury Diocese and the Wiltshire and Swindon History Centre, C/C/Bish/459/1.

which troublemakers trapped by their ankles could receive punishment through a public humiliation that likely included having refuse thrown at them. In 1647 the community at Kington Langley erected its own stocks, exasperated by the communal stocks of Kington being in a continual state of disrepair.

Another form of punishment was enacted in 1562 when a cucking stool was made. This device was essentially a chair, often resembling a commode, onto which someone, usually a woman (a scold, a woman who had spoken out of turn or cursed or slandered others), was strapped and paraded around the parish. It was hugely shameful for the recipient. Just six months after its construction, the parish cucking stool required repair. Whether this expedient was excessively used, thus necessitating the stool's early repair, is difficult to deduce.

An example of a cucking stool, from Wootton Bassett, used to punish and shame. Engraving published in Wilts Archaeological & Nat. Hist. Magazine, vol. 1, 1854.

During the medieval period, Kington St Michael sometimes also hosted the court of the hundred of North Damerham. At the hundred court of North Damerham cases from Nettleton, Grittleton, Christian Malford, and Kington St Michael (including Kington Langley) were heard. The hundred court usually sat twice yearly, although traditionally such courts met every three weeks. It may have been held in the open at St Michael's churchyard, under a particular tree or near the cross and market at Kington (the junction of Grove Lane and Honey Knob Hill), or under cover, perhaps in buildings owned by the abbey. The hundred court adjudicated on crimes that were more serious than those dealt with at the manor court. In 1480 representatives from Kington St Michael and Kington Langley attended the hundred court and reported tapsters (vendors of alcohol), brewers, a minor brawl and the prioress of St Mary's priory for failure to maintain local roads. As minor as these cases sound, the hundred court could also deal with cases of theft where individuals were found in possession of stolen goods, and, in such circumstances those convicted could be executed. Consequently, Kington St Michael had a gallows where those so deemed could, in theory, be hanged. How the judicial process would have worked in practice is open to conjecture. There is no evidence, for example, of a lock-up to hold prisoners before court proceedings or prior to such sentencing being carried out.

Surprisingly, it was the right of the prioress to raise the gallows on behalf of Kington St Michael, and not of Glastonbury abbey who owned most of the land. It was very unusual for a woman to have this right, and it afforded the prioress some status. The location of the gallows was described as a place where the lands of the abbey and priory were 'intermingled'. This was probably near the cross and market at Kington St Michael, but it could have been further south near Heywood farm or even elsewhere.

As the centuries passed, the importance of the manorial court (and hundred court) as places to deal with public order offences diminished. However, at Kington St Michael and Kington Langley the courts continued to sit into the late 19th century. In 1894 items discussed at the combined Kington St Michael and Kington Langley manor court

A person hanging from the gallows. Woodcut, 1790. Source: Wellcome Collection.

included consideration of who had felled a tree on Watling Street (Kington Langley), the regulation of ball games and the introduction of 6d. fines for those found removing dung from Langley common.

Case Study: The Langley Revel 1822

POSSIBLY THE BLOODIEST event in the history of the parish was the 'barbarous and blood-thirsty conflict' that occurred on 7 September 1822 between the men of 'Langley' (from Kington Langley and Langley Burrell) and the men of Chippenham. According to the *Devizes and Wiltshire Gazette* reporting several days later, the atrocity of the day's events was 'nearly unparalleled in English record.'

The affray occurred several weeks after the Kington Langley revel at which local men had become agitated at the conduct of several individuals from Chippenham. According to newspaper reports, after several 'skirmishes' between the men of Chippenham and Langley, it triggered a more significant retaliation by the men of Langley. Between 10 and 11 in the evening on 7 September, approximately 20–30 Langley men (40 in some reports) entered Chippenham 'armed with bludgeons and other weapons, when they assaulted and most dreadfully beat all persons they met without distinction.' The 'most respectable high constable' tried to appease the rioters but was beaten. The crowd's cries of 'murder' roused many from their beds, including Joseph Hull, a saddler. He was later found in 'a deplorable state' and died several hours afterwards. James Reynolds, brazier, was also found beaten, and he died three days later. In total, 31 were reported as injured in the affray. Twenty assailants, including two identified as ringleaders, were taken into custody. Those arrested were all men of Langley.

Witness testimony at the inquest (taken only from Chippenham residents) corroborated the press reporting and further recorded that the Langley men had been pushed out of town to just inside the boundary of Langley Burrell near the Little George public house. From here, they had then driven the larger group of Chippenham men back into the town. The inquest returned the verdict of 'wilful murder' against two farmers from Langley Burrell, John Matthews, of Barrow farm, and Henry Knight, and a number of others. However, just two labourers, George Thomas and Thomas Pearce, were called to trial. The rest were discharged on entering into recognisances to keep the peace.

The court was 'intensely crowded' during the trial of Thomas and Pearce. Several witnesses were called, but the case that the accused Langley men had caused murder was not proved, and they were acquitted.

A violent brawl. Detail from an etching by George Cruikshank, 1826, titled
Phrenological propensities: adhesiveness, inhabitiveness, constructiveness,
combativeness, destructiveness. Source: Wellcome Collection.

The reporting noted, 'There was very much rejoicing outside the court
when the result was made known to a number of Langley people, who
awaited with anxiety the fate of their neighbours.'

Over fifty years later, the diarist Francis Kilvert recorded a version
of events, informed by the testimony of Hannah and John Hatherall,
Langley Burrell residents who witnessed the revel. Kilvert's synopsis
varied slightly from the one reported at the time. Unsurprisingly perhaps,
as he was also the curate of Langley Burrell, he laid the blame for the
events with the town, stating, 'It was the fault of Chippenham. They began
it.' According to Kilvert, the men of Chippenham had long ill-used Langley
residents, beating local men on market days. The events of 7 September

had not been planned, but local men had decided to attend the market that day in force to avenge the usual insults. After some fighting, the Langley men withdrew as far as the Little George, next to the turnpike, where men from Chippenham taunted them. 'The Langley men, having gained their purpose and having drawn their enemies out of the town, now turned fiercely and charged upon them down the hill.' According to this version, 30 or 40 Langley men drove the 200-strong Chippenham mob 'before them like sheep.' 'The scene in the streets was fearful... But unhappily [alluding to the death of Hull and Reynolds] innocent men suffered with the guilty.' A day later, the courtyard at the brewery in Langley Burrell, where John Hatherall worked, was filled with people from Chippenham. Meanwhile constables combed the cottages of Langley for those suspected of being part of the riot. Kilvert noted that scarcely anyone from Chippenham was arrested and thus 'most of the blackguards got off scot-free.'

St Michael's church from Tor Hill, scene of demonstrations against the vicar in 1900. Early 20th century. From the collection of Tim Storer.

As surprising as it may seem, the murderous riot in 1822 that followed the Kington Langley revel was not the only occasion when Kington St Michael or Kington Langley were associated with an affray. In 1900 Britain was at war fighting in South Africa against the Boer republics of Transvaal and the Orange Free State. On 1 March the British had a significant success in the town of Ladysmith. It was a cause of celebration back home, but the patriotic fever in Kington St Michael was muted. The rector, Dr Adam Adrian, refused to allow the bells of the parish church to be rung in celebration. As the bells of surrounding churches pealed, it caused resentment within the village, and the parish bell ringers took to the streets ringing hand bells to show their frustration. On the following Sunday, an effigy of the vicar was found hanging from a tree overlooking the church.

However, this was mild compared to the reaction of people in Chippenham on hearing the news of Adrian (who was, by now, assumed to be a Boer sympathiser). On Monday, around 7 in the evening, a crowd started to leave Chippenham bound for Kington St Michael. Horns were blown, flags waved, songs sung, and tin pots were banged. A band made the journey too in a cart illuminated by Chinese lanterns. An effigy of the vicar was held aloft on a pole and 'hooted' by the crowd as it moved up the Malmesbury road towards the village. On reaching Kington, the procession, now 2–3000 strong by some reports, paraded up the main street following the band, cheering and singing as they went. After their return journey down the street, the crowd assembled on Tor Hill overlooking the vicarage. 'Combustibles' were drawn together and set alight with the effigy of Adrian on top. As the fire took hold, fireworks were thrown in and caused the flames to become brightly coloured. Crowds danced around the pyre as the band played. The effigy of the vicar was then dragged out of the fire and around the field. The crowd paraded again before a significant police presence encouraged them to disperse, still singing and cheering – thus ending the strange affair, but not before a stone smashed one of the vicarage windows.

When Adrian died in his post in 1906, he did not appear well mourned by his congregation or local bell-ringers. No mention was made of the events of March 1900 in his brief death notices in the newspapers, and the story of this revival of the old folk custom of 'rough music' was forgotten.

Coppieholders

...ington

...chard Ruffe coldeth a Tenement for his life — a ꝛ ꝓ
...and one in reversion paieing to it a garden cont — 0—0—10   li—s—d 0—10—0

...ice Ruffe widd coldeth one tenement for her life a ꝛ ꝓ
...choo in reversion with a garden Orchard &c — 0—3—34   li—s—d 0—15—0

...liam woeland coldeth for his wiues life one — 3—1ᵃ—1ʳ—30ᵖ   li—s—d 1—0—0
...in reversion And meadow with contayned

...omas Browne coldeth one tenement for his owne
life & one in reversion with hauz the ꝑticulars
...teroto belonging —

...his home close garden Orcharde barbefide is — a ꝛ ꝓ 0—3—30
...his pasture gr. bet No: Tobbire & y east feild is — 2—1—20
...his past. ground nere Tho: Smyth meade is — 3—3—32
...his past. ground bet Bowerlandes & Rich: Hawkins is — 4—0—24
...his little meade bet Tho: Smyth & Rich: Aros is — 0—3—3
...his Arr. at Quar by Rich: Aros is — 0—2—16
All his land in the foildis is — 9—3—28   li—s—
                                        Totall — 22ᵃ—2ʳ—33ᵖ   2—10—

...e Aland widd coldeth for her widdowhood one
tenement tow wth these ꝑticulars belongs — a ꝛ ꝓ
...her home close pasture garden Orcharde barbefide 1—3—15
...her Arr. close nere the East hammes — 2—2—20
...her meade below it — 2—1—20
...her Arr. close by the feild — 7—0—14
...her Arra: close below that — 5—3—23
...her Arra: close called hurstlandes — 8—1—20
...her Meade bet John fryst & her owne land is — 1—3—0
...her land adioyning to her land Southward — 0—2—16
All her land in the ffoildis is — 2—3—4   li—
                                        Totall — 33ᵃ—1ʳ—12ᵖ   0—

...ne Aland widd holdeth ffor her widdowhood one — a ꝛ ꝓ
life in reversion one close Arr. by Oorbis cont 7—2—20   hir

...omas Gingell coldeth for his life & one in reversion — 7ᵃ—0ʳ—0ᵖ   v—
...his close of pasture nere the east feild being

                  All the land on this fide is — 72ᵃ—2ʳ—19ᵖ   tot   li
                                                              12

The regulation of minor public order offences was only one aspect of the work of the manor court in the medieval and early modern period. Most of its business involved organising land tenure (for example, to pass a tenanted farm from father to son). Aside from tithingmen (local petty constables) and affeerors (who determined the fines payable by local transgressors), the local manor court selected other officers such as waywardens or highway surveyors who were responsible for the upkeep of local roads, and field supervisors who were tasked with maintaining boundaries. After the manor of Kington St Michael (which included Kington Langley) was divided among the heirs of Charles Snell in 1656, the manor court was also divided, with at least one inheriting party holding a separate court for their third. This highly distinctive arrangement was extremely unusual and probably illegal, but it continued nonetheless for two centuries.

From the 17th century another form of local government was developed, the parish vestry. A 'vestry' was a parish committee that

Above: A satirist's view of a vestry meeting. Coloured etching by Thomas Rowlandson, 1806. Source: The Metropolitan Museum of Art, New York.
Previous page: Sample from a manor survey in 1655 survey showing typical tenant holdings. Reproduced courtesy of the Wiltshire and Swindon History Centre, 873/140.

traditionally met in the church vestry after worship and dealt with poor relief, highways, and more. The use of this mechanism began in many English places during the 16th century when the government was compelled to legislate to fill a void in local government created by the dissolution of the monasteries. The traditional 'manor' was also on the wane. In Kington St Michael including Kington Langley, it is most likely that the vestry committee was formed during the mid-17th century to deal with the problem of poverty. As highlighted in the chapter 'Social life, Superstition, Schools and Support', the villages raised a locally collected tax called poor rates, which was used to cover the cost of welfare. As the local manors became divided and the population began to rise, so the role the manor courts took in local government became weak. Although Kington Langley was part of the parish of Kington St Michael until the 1860s, by the early 1800s evidence suggests that, although the selection of officers was sometimes endorsed at the Kington St Michael vestry until 1855, residents of Kington Langley were organising welfare and probably road maintenance separately from the rest of the parish.

From the mid-1850s the parish vicar, Edward Awdry, dominated the vestry committee. Parish officers were selected every year, and under Awdry's chairmanship the roles were chosen from the same few men. Officers included overseers (who collected poor rates), churchwardens (who looked after the church and were *de facto* overseers), and highway surveyors or waywardens. Postholders were usually designated to cover either the tithing of Easton Piercy or Kington St Michael. In addition to the regular office holders, from 1860 two collectors and assessors of taxes were selected, and in 1861 two constables for Kington St Michael and one for Easton Piercy were nominated. The post of parish constable was more arduous than the previous role of tithingman but was very part-time, in that a constable was only required to work in his parish and only should the need arise. The effectiveness of these officers relied heavily on their public spiritedness and physical ability. Their number was reduced to two in 1863 when the constables were Charles Dyer (wheelwright) for Kington St Michael and David Blake (farmer) for Easton Piercy. The following year only Dyer was retained. The number of officers continued to fluctuate until 1870, presumably as the need and inclination rose and fell. In 1874, the use of parish-appointed constables nationwide was abolished, by which time their use locally had come

Herbert Prodgers, squire of Kington St Michael and prominent member of the vestry committee. Camille Silvy albumen print, 14 June 1862. Source: National Portrait Gallery, Ax58579.

to an end. Later, in the early 20th century, a police station was established in the village by Wiltshire County Constabulary.

Another prominent name on the vestry from the 1860s onwards was that of Herbert Prodgers. Prodgers' father died in 1861, leaving him a substantial inheritance with which he bought the manor house in Kington St Michael. On the death of his mother in 1863, he inherited further money. It enabled him to play the role of the squire successfully, and in that year he demolished the manor house and rebuilt it. By reputation, Prodgers is characterised as having had disagreements with the vicar (and vestry chair), and so built the gatehouse at the entrance to his drive adjacent to St Michael's church, and this enabled him, so the story goes, to sit and hear the Sunday service without actually having to enter the church. Yet evidence from the vestry minutes highlights Prodgers' continuous participation on the vestry committee from 1864 and (broadly) does not imply any rift. Instead, he was seen as a benefactor to the village. In a meeting on 25 February 1869, 'The meeting gave thanks to Mr. Prodgers for his liberality in erecting a schoolhouse and teacher's residence for the instruction of poor children of the parish.' At the same time consent was also apparently given to Prodgers 'to take away the upper part of the walk of the churchyard' near his entrance. This was a move that should have required the consent of the bishop.

The Kington St Michael parish council was formed in 1894 and consisted of six councillors. The first minute book has been lost but was the subject of a short article in the local press in 1938, which suggested that the government of the parish continued in the hands of a small clique.

The communities of Kington St Michael and Kington Langley had primarily been administered together since 1189, but by the 19th century the villages had developed distinct community identities. This feeling appears to have become more intense after the creation of the church of St Peter's at Kington Langley in 1857. On 17 April 1865, a memorandum was passed around the vestry meeting at Kington St Michael stating that Kington Langley (as Langley Fitzurse) had been made an ecclesiastical district by Queen Victoria. The following year Kington Langley became a civil parish. Thereafter, until its abolition in 1894, no further mention was made of Kington Langley at the Kington St Michael vestry meetings, with one exception which became divisive. The Lyte almshouses in Kington St Michael were, in principle, also available to poor men in Kington Langley. Consequently Charles Clarke, vicar of St. Peter's, made a plea at the Kington St Michael vestry meeting on 19 May 1883 for one of his parishioners, William Halbert, to be elected to a place in the almshouses. However, Prodgers, had other ideas and nominated Jesse Alderman from Kington St. Michael to fill the vacancy. There was a discussion followed by a vote, and each man received two votes; this left the casting vote to the vicar of St Michael's, Edward Awdry, who opted in a conciliatory fashion in favour of William Halbert.

After 1866 Kington Langley was responsible for its local government, which necessitated the creation of its own vestry committee. No doubt this was a joyous and welcome development, but the first annual Kington Langley parish meeting in 1867 became divisive. During the proceedings, local 'dissenters', including the Baptist minister Jeremiah Ashe, attempted to subvert the proceedings by suppressing the churchwardens' accounts and refusing the church rate (a locally raised tax to provide funds to support the parish church). Church rates were, according to Ashe and friends, 'an unwanted assumption of ecclesiastical tyranny.' Much animosity was probably directed at the vicar, John Jeremiah Daniell, who had written a pamphlet in support of compulsory church rates, *A Solemn Cry Concerning Church Rates*. Daniell suggested that curtailing church rates was akin to robbing God. Despite the tempers, Ashe's attempt failed and the incident was reported in the local newspapers with a certain amount of tutt-tutting. Luckily, nationwide compulsory church rates were abolished in 1868, and Ashe and his friends happily became part of the committee and served as elected parish officers.

Case Study: Kington St Michael in the Second World War

Insignia of the Home Guard. ©
IWM (INS 7379)

THE KINGTON ST MICHAEL platoon of the Home Guard, part of G Company of the 1st Chippenham Battalion, formed in May 1940, was under the command of Major (George) Malcolm Thompson of the manor, Kington St Michael. The platoon comprised 44, probably more mature men, many of whom like Thompson had seen action in the First World War. Their role, particularly after the fall of Dunkirk on 5 June 1940, was to form part of the defence of the country in the event of an invasion. Major Thompson was also the chair of the Kington St Michael Invasion Committee, which was tasked to plan what the wider response of the community should be if Germany invaded. Throughout most of the war, Thompson was chair of the parish council too. Thompson gave more than his time to the war effort, he made available his motorcar in the event of an emergency in the village and his stables for the reception of fatal casualties should the worst happen.

The Kington invasion committee was made up of men and women. Unsurprisingly, however, in the allocation of tasks there was a division of labour, except in the relaying of messages, when both sexes got involved. Mrs Thompson (of the manor) was allocated food and charge of the Women's Voluntary Service while Mrs Stanley Lee and several other women took charge of first aid. The first aid point was the schoolroom at the Bethesda chapel, now a private house. Men were fire wardens, fire fighters and Home Guards. The chief fire warden was Philip du Cros of Bolehyde manor. Ordinary fire warden, Stanley Lee, ran the village stores on the street (he is listed in *Kelly's Directory* as a grocer, draper and 'wireless apparatus dealer'). His stores served as the fire wardens' post.

By June 1940 a Kington fire brigade had also been formed under Mr Taylor of West View. Taylor was also responsible for billeting evacuees. The fire brigade initially comprised six men and two manual pumps, a standpipe and 50 ft hose. Dudley Isaac's car and trailer were to be used to transport the pumps to the scene of the fire should the need arise. As the war progressed more men volunteered, and more equipment was acquired.

A survey was carried out of Kington farms on behalf of the Ministry of Agriculture and Fisheries in 1943. Many farms had given over pasture to crop production during the previous years to help meet the nation's demand for home-produced food. At Kington manor, head of the local invasion response, home guard and parish council, Major Thompson (who was also agricultural liaison officer to the county's agricultural committee) had given over 7 acres for oats in 1940 and a further 5 acres to oats and 8 acres to wheat the following year. His management was classified as 'A'. Most but not all local farmers were likewise approved. 'The farmer is getting on in years and has let the farm get into rather a dilapidated state' was the assessment of one whose arable cultivation was deemed 'especially poor'.

The women of the WI were actively involved in the war effort too. At their monthly meeting in August 1940, at which Miss Gowring gave a talk on her travels in New Zealand, it was reported that the Working

A group of Home Guard are trained in the use of a Northover Projector 'somewhere in England, 1941' © IWM (D 4357).

She's in the Ranks too !

CARING FOR EVACUEES IS A NATIONAL SERVICE

ISSUED BY THE MINISTRY OF HEALTH

Information Poster by Ministry of Information © IWM (Art.IWM PST 8561)

Party's Red Cross fund had collected half a ton of wastepaper, tins and
jars. The money raised was used to purchase wool, and volunteers then
knitted 'comforts' – items for sick and wounded soldiers and prisoners
of war. By December, they had produced 130 pairs of pyjamas, 59 pairs
of socks, 34 bed jackets, 24 dressing gowns plus shirts, helmets, socks,
mittens and gloves. Funds were also raised for the WI Ambulance Fund.
A National Savings group of the WI encouraged women to invest in
National Savings, that directly supported the government's war effort. In
1941, according to the WI reminiscences of Barbara Taylor, the women
of the WI combined with the local home guard and provided a float in
the (Chippenham?) Carnival, no doubt to raise more money for the war
effort. Later speakers at the Kington St Michael WI meetings delivered
talks designed to instruct the women on growing produce and cooking
'war-time dishes'. Along with other groups the Kington WI set about
making jam to contribute to national food supplies, and at Christmas they
sent gifts to local servicemen.

　　Throughout the war the patriotic community of Kington raised
funds. Amongst many others, in October 1942 a dance was organised in
aid of the British Prisoners of War Fund, an organisation set up to provide
books and games for prisoners in Germany and Italy. In November 1943
a whist drive was held for the Red Cross.

　　At the school, now the village hall, the children's education was
predictably impacted by the war. School numbers rose with the arrival of
evacuees from London boroughs, including Enfield and Ealing. Seventeen
evacuees were on the school roll before war had even broken out. The
total had risen to 25 by July 1940 and significantly bolstered school
numbers, which before the war had been falling. A J Harcourt, a teacher
from Alma Rd School, Enfield, assisted teachers at Kington for many
months, likely providing a valuable link to home for many of the children.
However, the school struggled for space, staff and warmth during the
winter months, when the inadequate heating forced its closure on a
number of occasions.

　　The war affected the school in far more ways than just the
arrival of evacuees. For the managers of the school, for example, war
necessitated plans for tackling fire in the event of enemy action. Sandbags
were provided as the first line of defence. In the event of the failure of the
main water supply to feed the parish's own fire engine, the old rainwater

tank above the toilets and the village pond were to be used as alternative sources of water. But, despite requests, the education authority refused to provide buckets. Pupils were given gas masks that required regular inspection. In 1943 complaints were made to managers that army lorries had been backing and turning in the school playground. Surprisingly it was decided that fencing the playground would be more dangerous than leaving the space open for encroachment by army vehicles.

School holidays were adapted, often staggered, or extended, during hostilities to allow children to work on the land, especially at harvest time when the local labour shortage was particularly acute. Even during term-time children were sometimes given dispensation to help out. In one instance during a week in October 1942, all pupils over the age of 12 were given leave of absence by the Director of Education to go potato picking 'whereby the school lost 64 attendances.' The school garden was turned over to the cultivation of vegetables, including cabbages and potatoes, to help feed the nation – the education authority providing the children with garden tools. Children helped in the war effort in other ways too, such as by collecting paper salvage for the paper mill at Slaughterford.

Despite these measures, there was still some time for the children to have fun. In February 1944 the school had a delayed Christmas party, and children were presented with boxes of sweets by American soldiers, possibly stationed at the base in nearby Langley Burrell. At the parish council, despite the wartime planning, business in some respects continued as normal with the usual complaints over bad smells from local drains and inconveniences caused by overhanging hedges.

The cessation of hostilities in Europe in 1945 brought communal celebrations. These involved a service of thanksgiving, but also, no doubt, late night merrymaking – as pupils returning to school on 11 May 1945 after two days of community celebrations were found too tired to do any work. A 'Welcome Home' fete was organised in early August in the grounds of the manor house in aid of the Welcome Home Society, to provide certificates and money to returning soldiers. Even before VE day the parish council was looking to the future and, probably mindful of the return of demobbed soldiers, wrote to the Rural District Council to ask that more homes be built within the village.

At the first meeting of the Kington Langley parish council on 4 December 1894, nine parish councillors were chosen. Initially, the council met at the school and largely discussed routine matters such as appointing parish officers, managing charities, and maintaining local footpaths. In exasperation, possibly at the inactivity of the parish council where the issue had already been raised, the vicar's wife wrote to the district council on a different topic in 1895 asking if anything could be done to prevent the community from being 'poisoned by fearfully bad smells in the village resulting from pigs'. An inspector was sent around and made several orders for work by local pig keepers, including taking steps to keep them in more sanitary conditions.

However objectionable the pigs may have been, the twin issues of water supply (from local wells) and sanitation became the pre-eminent problem of the early decades of the Kington Langley parish council. The village ponds were sometimes used as receptacles for wastewater, and water quality, when tested, was unsatisfactory. However, at first, the parish council resisted the imperative to act, and in November 1909 they reported to the district council that they had received no negative reports about the quality of the supply. In 1910, the county medical officer took 60 water samples across the parish and declared the entire supply unfit for human consumption. In the words of the medical officer, John Tubb Thomas, 'many of the samples have all the appearance of effluents from a sewage farm; hardly a single sample is free from objectionable odour when heated and all swarm with organisms.' Even the squire W T Coleman's supply was 'very, very bad.' Despite this, the parish council remained reticent. Two years later a water pipe was laid to connect the village to the Chippenham reservoir at Hardenhuish. In 1915 a sanitary committee was formed. After the First World War the council focused on improving local sanitation and water supply. They also recognised the need for new housing, an issue which, following the Second World War, was again a significant issue.

Case Study: Kington Langley in the Second World War

K INGTON LANGLEY'S preparations for war began early in 1939. Volunteers from Kington Langley and surrounding villages attended a first aid training course held in the village hall – part of civil plans in the event of air raids.

At Old Chapel Fields, a little later in the year, Robin and Heather Tanner adopted Dietrich Hanff, a Jewish teenager from Stettin, north Germany. He settled in well. However, in early summer 1940, Robin and Heather were awoken by an air raid siren and, 20 minutes later, heard explosions from two bombs landing at a farm several miles away. The sound woke Dietrich, and they read him *Through the Looking Glass* for several hours to soothe his agitation. Robin wrote, 'That has been our only experience so far'. 'Most of our village slept through its warning and heard no bombs!'

The serenity of the village changed through that summer, so that by July, soldiers were 'everywhere' in Kington Langley.

Dietrich Hanff, from An Exceptional Woman: the Writings of Heather Tanner, *Hobnob Press, 2006*

And, Robin noted, 'I am battling today with a major who wants to take my garage. He will win, I suppose.' In that month, Dietrich or Dieti as he was then known, was taken by the authorities to an internment camp, and Old Chapel Field was searched for bombs. It caused the Tanners some anguish. Dieti returned to his Langley home full-time in November 1942 and, to the delight of the Tanners, spent the rest of the war studying at home and gardening.

Dietrich was not the only child evacuated to the village. In June 1939, 18 children from London were billeted with families across the parish, and they were joined by another 12 three months later. Betty Bird recalls her family taking in a mother and daughter from Bermondsey. Kathleen was a few years younger than Betty, and they became like sisters.

At first the evacuees were taught separately in the infant classroom at the village school, but were soon integrated with the rest. The following January, schoolchildren aged between 4 and 10 and locally billeted evacuees were thrown a party. Each child had a present, sweets, and an orange donated by Mrs White of the Limes. As welcome as these events may have been, organising and integrating evacuees into school life was complicated. Robin Tanner, a local school inspector, observed so much chaos in the county's schools, and wrote, 'I find it hard to look forward to any sort of system or stability again'.

In common with other local schools, the holidays in Kington Langley were adjusted, particularly the summer break, so that children could help during harvest. In 1941 the holiday was staggered from 15 August to 8 September and then from 26 September to 13 October, when potatoes were harvested. Betty Bird, whose father was the gardener at Great House, spent her summers employed in killing Cabbage White butterflies to stop them laying eggs and producing caterpillars that would feed on the produce.

Wartime information poster © IWM (Art.IWM PST 15106)

As in many other years, there were the occasional outbreaks of childhood illnesses. In 1941 measles caused a significant problem. On 18 March only 21 out of 53 children on the roll were in school. The outbreak continued to affect attendance for many weeks to come, so school was cancelled altogether during several weeks during March and April. But, there were also problems with wartime supplies. On 20 February 1941 the school sent home pupils as 'coke supplies have been exhausted' and the building was freezing. These problems persisted through the rest of the year.

The Kington Langley WI had its first meeting in early 1939. After the outbreak of war, its efforts were focused on aiding the war effort and the group promoted wartime savings and collected tins and wastepaper to raise funds for comforts for troops. The meeting lapsed by the end of 1941. However, a fruit preserving centre was established at Kington Langley during the early months of the war, drawing the efforts of many former members and those from neighbouring branches. The centre contributed to nationwide efforts to bolster food supplies and help to ensure surplus fruit was not wasted. Fruit from the surrounding area, much of it organised by the local WIs, was sent to Kington Langley for

Women's Institute members at a jam-making centre on the east coast of England © IWM (D 4857)

preserving, bottling and canning. By November 1940, two tons of jam had been made, and much more fruit had been bottled or canned.

Local farmers were encouraged to plough over pasture and plant grain and produce so as to increase domestic food production. It was not just local farmers. At the Great House, the 7-acre garden was given over to horticultural produce. It included strawberries, raspberries, loganberries, gooseberries, and blackcurrants. Its owner, the widowed, Mrs Garnett, was rated a grade 'A' farmer. At the Manor House and Langley Ridge, the gardens were let to local farmers and given over to pasture during the summer months. Their occupiers were, like Mrs Garnett, commended. However, not all local agriculturalists earned praise – several merited lesser accolades. One was characterised by the National Farm Survey in 1943 as an 'easy going and unenterprising farmer inclined to "muddle along"'. Another farmer was 'inclined to be lazy.'

Wartime information poster to get women involved in armaments manufacture © IWM (Art. IWM PST 17422)

Whatever the perceived personal failings of some within the community, more broadly the efforts across the parish, including the donation of food for Chippenham hospital and the scrap metal collections of 'Freddie House and his little friends', prompted the *Wiltshire Times and Trowbridge Advertiser* to comment in August 1940, 'it would appear that most of the village are engaged on war work of one type or another.' These efforts would continue, the village having its own 'Waste Paper Salvage

Committee' in 1943. However, not everyone embraced the war effort similarly, and several residents were given military exemptions on the grounds of their conscientious objections.

Some aspects of village war work were clandestine (or supposed to be). At Church farm, aside from helping with food production, there was a secret depot operated by Westinghouse Brake & Signal Co. where women were principally working assembling rectifier units 'for war service on land, sea and in the air'. While it appears that the community was aware that war work was going on at the farm, few knew its exact nature.

The village platoon of the Home Guard was much more visible to the community. In 1941, along with Kington St Michael Platoon, they had the honour of representing German forces in a home guard exercise at Sutton Benger, and 'gained initial success and obtained control of part of the village before reinforcements arrived and drove them out.' The exercise, which included 'a gas attack, without gas' and simulated machine gun fire, was designed to test the resources of local villages to enemy attack. It drew large crowds of local spectators.

Despite everything, however, in some ways life was normal; the hounds of the Duke of Beaufort regularly met at Kington Langley, the harvest festival continued to be celebrated, weekly dances took place in the village hall (albeit in support of local men in the forces) and the parish council appeared largely preoccupied with parochial issues. In 1944,

The Home Guard on a training exercise 'somewhere in England, 1941' somewhere in England, 1941 © IWM (D 4359)

the parish council wrote to the county council over three issues: the height of the Tanners' hedge at Old Chapel Field, refuse being dumped by residents opposite Old Chapel Field, and the dangerous state of the bridge on 'Church Path'.

When news reached Kington Langley of the allied victory over Japan in August 1945 the weekly dance was taking place at the village hall. Mr and Mrs Bence hurried over with the intelligence. The Blue Aces Dance Band, who had been playing, left the hall and started to parade through the village, dancing followed on the Common probably until well into the night. The next week, festivities of a less spontaneous nature took place. Alongside sports and games, there was a picnic on the common organised by Nora and Pearl Parnell, sisters who had organised the village's weekly dances to raise money for local people serving in the forces. A few days later, the Parnell sisters were the focus of a poison pen letter sent to their father, who kept the village stores. 'Everyone in the village is talking about you and wondering to whom the money goes. It is well known you are doing it for custom and self-glorification. Why the heck don't you be sports and hand over the money.' After a meeting, the village publicly endorsed the work of the sisters in the press, sending a message to the writer that their behaviour would not be tolerated.

The Lyte Almshouses c.1847. Sketch given to John Jackson by John Britton.
Reproduced courtesy of the Society of Antiquaries, London, JAC 006.

4

SOCIAL LIFE SUPERSTITION SCHOOLS & SUPPORT

FOR CENTURIES NO-ONE was particularly wealthy in the villages of Kington St Michael and Kington Langley. Taxation records from the medieval and Tudor periods indicate that the parish was a community of agriculturalists and no one paid a large amount of tax. Before the dissolution of the monasteries in the mid-16th century the wealthiest inhabitants with the highest social status were the prioress of St Mary's, Glastonbury abbey's estate bailiff, the owner of Easton Piercy and the vicar of St Michael's church. The communal life of the parish was centred largely on the church, particularly Christian feast days.

St Michael's church in 1907. From the collection of Tim Storer.

Significant revels took place at Kington's three-day fair held at Michaelmas, the festival of St. Michael the Archangel, that took place on 29 September. Local people celebrated the end of harvest, ate fattened geese, and drank ale. According to John Aubrey, writing in the 17th century, it was much resorted to by the young, implying they drank heavily. However, while the events at St Michael's were undoubtedly joyous, at Kington Langley Aubrey described the revel as 'one of the greatest Revells in these parts.' The revel, likely associated with the dedication of St Peter's chapel, was celebrated on the Sunday following the feast of St Peter (29 June). Aubrey recounted that such festivities traditionally took place in the parish church house (a building akin to a village hall) where following a night of fasting and praying, officers were chosen for gathering money for charitable uses. He described Old John Wastfield of Langley informing him he had been 'Peterman', undoubtedly a name for the Langley alms collector at the revels, during the reign of Elizabeth I. The celebration probably took place within the chapel rather than an associated building. After the chapel had been converted into a cottage in the mid-17th century the annual revels continued but they became entirely disassociated with religion and almsgiving and more about drinking and having fun. It is likely that the only play Aubrey wrote, *The Countrey Revell*, which only survives in fragments, and features 'Squire Fitz-Ale' and a drunken vigil at the feast of St Peter was a parody of the annual event in Kington Langley.

In 1791 a teenager died after a fight broke out at the revel. Later, in 1822, the event precipitated a major riot. By this time the revel was associated with 'Langley'- both Kington Langley and Langley Burrell. The affray, as we described more fully in the previous chapter, occurred weeks after the event, at which some local offence was taken at the conduct of several individuals from Chippenham. During the evening of 7 September, approximately 20-30 Langley men (40 in some reports) entered Chippenham 'armed with bludgeons and other weapons, when they assaulted and most dreadfully beat all persons they met without distinction.' Two men died and 31 were injured in the affray. Twenty assailants, including two identified as ringleaders, were taken into custody.

Another important date at the parish church in Kington during the medieval and Tudor periods was the 'church ale' at Whitsun, the seventh Sunday after Easter, probably held in the church yard at St Michael's. Here householders met, drank ale and gave charity while young people danced, bowled and practised their archery skills. Communal celebrations at village weddings could also be significant too. When Aubrey was young he observed a local wedding celebration at the crossroads next to the pound in Easton Piercy at which young men rode horses and attempted to strike a target with a truncheon, this was called a quintain. The quintain comprised an upright post on which was a cross beam, at one end of which was hanging a leather satchel filled with sand and at the other end was a piece of wood 'that turnes on the pinne of the rowler'. The men gave the target a 'lusty bang' with their truncheons but had to beware. Aubrey observed that: 'If they [were] not cunning in it and nimble, the Sand-bag takes them in ye powle'. It 'twas a pretty rustique sport.' The tradition of the quintain did not survive after the English civil war.

We also know from local records that local people across both Kington St Michael and Kington Langley enjoyed themselves in other ways throughout the year. They played ball games, frequented local alehouses and had access to Glastonbury abbey's deer park, which ranged south from their grange (the site of the present manor at Kington St Michael). Village life was probably enlivened at other times by travellers to the priory and the abbey grange. The visits of the wealthy abbot of Glastonbury accompanied by a large retinue to enjoy hunting in the park or of the bishop to the priory were likely to have been particularly noteworthy.

Rider tilting at a replica quintain of Offham Green in Kent in 1976. In public domain via Wikimedia commons.

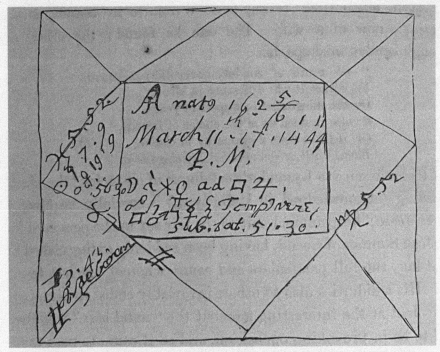

Horoscope of the birth of John Aubrey. Sketched from Aubrey's original by John Jackson. Source: Wiltshire Archaeological & Nat. Hist. Magazine, *vol. 4 (1858).*

Case Study: Superstition and Folklore

THE 17TH-CENTURY ANTIQUARY John Aubrey believed in witchcraft, magic and astrology. He was born in Kington St Michael in 1626, and reading his work with its many references to his childhood home suggests that everyone in the community felt similarly. He recounted how local people left offerings to fairies next to their hearths and that when he was a boy the maids used ashes in the hearth to divine who they should marry. People kissed their hands and bowed to a new moon for luck. He described the area as forever having been associated with witches, and remembered seeing ghostly shadows with several other gentlemen while a guest at Kington manor in December 1653.

Writing over 150 years later, John Britton, also born in the parish, reflected that most inhabitants still remained 'sincere and ardent believers in the appearance of ghosts, in haunted houses, in witchcraft, in necromancy, in fairies, and their manufactory of grass rings, in the supernatural influence of Jack-a-lanterns, or will-o'-the-wisps, and many other visionary vagaries, which belonged not merely to the lower and middle, but to the educated and higher classes of society.'

Will-o'-the-Wisp. A mirage in a marsh. Coloured wood engraving by C. Whymper (1853-1941). Source: Wellcome Collection.

Although in later life Britton was dismissive of such beliefs, in his youth he had been just as affected by them, recounting his dread of walking through the churchyard or by a house (not named) reputed to have been haunted. Britton sometimes let the family pony loose in the road rather than take her into her field as he was so fearful of ghosts and Jack-a-lanterns (Jack, a ghostly folk figure, roamed the world with a lantern carved from a turnip illuminated by a red-hot ember from hell).

These beliefs continued into the 19th century, if not beyond. John Jackson recorded several ghosts in 1860, including the spirit of the 'vulgar sot' and lord of the manor of Kington, Ayliffe White. One unnamed Kington woman who knew White in life felt it was no surprise that he had returned, as when people died they 'did come back', and such apparitions were 'quite nat'ral like.'

Many local customs were concerned with love and death. The maids of Aubrey's youth 'would stick up midsummer-men' into the chinks of building joists. These midsummer-men were sprigs of a plant (a species of Sedum) that Aubrey called 'orphins'. These sprigs were placed in pairs 'one for such a man, the other for such a maid his sweetheart, and accordingly as the orphin did incline to, or recline from the other, that there would be love or aversion.' If the sprigs withered, it signified a death. Two hundred years later, Francis Kilvert recounted his mother who had been born in Kington told him that, in her youth, maids and 'cottage girls' stuck "Midsummer Men" up in their houses and bedrooms on Midsummer Eve 'for the purpose of divining about their sweethearts'.

Aubrey also observed that it was a custom for people 'that were more curious than ordinary' to sit all night in the church porch on Midsummer's Eve 'and they should see the apparitions of those that should die in the parish that year come and knock at the dore'. Aubrey himself had some experience of the knocking of the dead. Just before his father died, as he was lying in bed, Aubrey heard three knocks on his bedhead. His father was buried in St Michael's church at Kington.

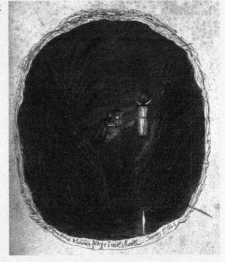

Also buried in St Michael's church in the 17th century was a 'practitioner of physic' or 'emperick', seemingly a folk healer, a John Power. The enigmatic Power appears in Aubrey's manuscripts several times. In his topographical description of north Wiltshire, Aubrey records that Power was buried 'arsy varsy' in the south aisle of the church. The burial was topsy-turvy, upside-down, the wrong way round – a manner contrary to what was usual. Being buried in this way, and seemingly without a memorial, had implications. Power may have been buried upside-down to stop

Jack-a-Lantern as a demon standing among bullrushes at the water's edge at night and holding a lantern. Etching by G. Cruikshank, 1842. Source: Wellcome Collection.

An alchemist hunched over his crucible. Coloured lithograph by Bouvier, 1830, after J. Steen 1626-1679. Source: Wellcome Collection.

his corpse from rising again to trouble the living.

One religious writer later suggested that Power's practice in physic was a cover for a study of alchemy 'or the still darker mystery of the Black-Art'. There may be some truth: Power attended Gloucester Hall, Oxford at the same time as the astrologer, mathematician and suspected magician and necromancer, Thomas Allen. Power fed Aubrey stories of Allen, although it is not clear whether the two were personally acquainted. Pseudo-physicians of the period, like Power, often used astrology in their practice, and as with Allen, these aspects could be used in conjunction with other things. Gloucester Hall, Oxford did not enforce strict religious conformity either, and in such an environment Power probably studied things which he later practised at home in Kington. Power's family had some history in this area too. His uncle had been a 'chymist'. This was a subject in its infancy and many chymists were engaged in alchemy, including the father of modern chemistry, Robert Boyle. Power learned things from his uncle, (Thomas?) Penn, and also recounted them to Aubrey. Back in the village, the lord of the manor, Thomas Snell, who died in 1612, and his son, Charles, who died in 1651, were noted astrologers. Perhaps the local environment was conducive to the study of the dark arts. At the time of Power's death, England was in the social and political turmoil of the Civil War, and accusations of witchcraft were reaching a peak. Regular religious and civil government was interrupted. Unfortunately, Aubrey kept quiet about certain things – after all, he may have hoped to publish his manuscript – and we are thus unlikely to learn the full circumstances of Power's death.

After the dissolution, for many living in Kington St Michael and Kington Langley it may have felt that not much had changed as the former estate bailiff, Richard Snell, whose family had held that position for generations, bought the manor of Kington from Henry VIII. However, this was soon to change; villagers were no longer allowed to access the park, and gradually the Snell family enclosed land formerly communally held, despite opposition from their tenants. Nicholas Snell demolished Glastonbury abbey's grange and built a new manor house. His meteoric rise was assisted by a judicious marriage to Alice, daughter of John Pye of Rowden, which promoted him from the lower ranks of the minor gentry to become an MP for Chippenham and sheriff of Wiltshire. The Snells' behaviour to their neighbours and the Crown, as well as to the Kington community, indicates that

Kington St Michael manor erected on the site of Glastonbury abbey's grange. The manor was demolished during the 1860s.
Reproduced courtesy of the Society of Antiquaries, London, JAC 006.

they enjoyed their wealth and were ruthlessly ambitious. There is evidence that Nicholas Snell financially abused the weak-willed Andrew Bayntun of the manors of Rowden and Stanley, relieving Bayntun of his property at a knockdown price. Nicholas and his son, John, were also clearly complicit in defrauding the Crown in their lease of the manor of West Hatch, yet both avoided severe censure.

Social life in the villages under the Snells no doubt carried on much as it had done before the reformation. At the manor court several brewers were regularly fined (a *de facto* form of local licensing). Drinking alcohol was considered a gateway to all manner of other vices and misbehaviour. Those so 'licensed' were occasionally fined for allowing illicit games or drinking after hours. Gambling was considered a problem for the moral health of the community, and so were the organised games of staff-ball and football that evidently sometimes took young men away from church on Sundays.

The reign of the Snells was eventually curtailed when Charles Snell died without children in the 1650s and the manor of Kington was divided among his sisters. This division of the estate, and the fact that the vicar was often no longer resident in the parish, meant that no 'gentleman' was likely to be living in the community. The villages were still largely made up of families earning their living from the land and the rhythm of rural life continued as it had for centuries, but the village became quieter. John Aubrey born in Kington in 1626, described a childhood of 'eremiticall solitude', one isolated from the outside world.

A century on and John Britton born in 1771 recalled the Kington St Michael of his youth as quiet and dull, speculating that no inhabitant was likely to have even purchased a newspaper or magazine before 1780. In his account the village was periodically brightened by the visits of a clothier and a particular 'Mountebank Doctor'. This 'itinerant quack' had a companion called 'Merry-Andrew', 'a sort of clown, or buffoon, whose office and duty was to submit to the horse-whip, to tumble, leap, dance, make grotesque faces, and parley badinage and vulgar jokes with his equally accomplished master.' He went further, 'Without a regular churchman to advise and admonish, or a magistrate, or private gentleman residing in the principal house of the village, the inhabitants were undisciplined, illiterate, and deprived of all good example; whilst those who were constitutionally

An itinerant medicine vendor (a mountebank doctor) selling his wares with the aid of a monkey and a performer dressed as harlequin. Engraving.
Source: Wellcome Collection.

idle and dissipated had no check on their conduct and became too often promoters of bad habits in the young.' This was somewhat unfair given that Britton also recounted he had fished in the carp ponds of Kington manor as a boy trespassing and consequently had once narrowly avoided being shot by Squire White.

Things came somewhat more culturally highbrow during the Victorian period when Edward Awdry became vicar, and the manor was purchased by Herbert Prodgers. It meant that in the 1850s and 1860s the manor house and school at Kington St Michael were demolished and rebuilt, slum dwellings were pulled down, including Britton's childhood home, and St Michael's church was 'renovated'. Both Awdry and Prodgers took a keen interest in local affairs, including Kington's cultural life. Yet the village remained slightly removed from the bustle of the outside world. The Victorian diarist Francis Kilvert described visiting Awdry on New Year's Day 1875.

As I neared the village the tall brown Church Tower rose over the snowy waste with its pinnacles and delicate balustrade, the wind was roaring through the yielding boughs of the four trees that crown the Tor Hill. In the fading afternoon light the trees bent and swayed black against the leaden grey sky and the white slopes beyond. It was a strange dreary altered scene. The village was silent.

Silver Street, Kington Langley early 20th century. From the collection of Tim Storer.

Meanwhile at Kington Langley during the 1850s Canon John Jackson was disdainful of local goings on, characterising the village in these terms: 'this distance from clerical superintendence and the wholesome discipline of Church and School, having been found to produce the usual ill effects of ignorance and irreligion, testified by numerous and increasing cases brought before magistrates and boards of guardians, as well as by Sabbath breaking and irregularities of various kinds.' Typical of these activities was the riot at the revels in 1822. No doubt some of these effects were caused by alcohol. The village had a long tradition of drinking places, with four innkeepers recorded in the village in 1739. The Plough inn, Plough Lane, sadly closed by 2018, was established by 1768 and was the only inn in Kington Langley marked on Andrews and Dury's map of Wiltshire in 1773. In 1853 the sign outside

Scene outside the Plough Inn, Kington Langley early 20th century. From the collection of Tim Storer.

it read, 'In hope we Plough: In hope we sow; By hope we all are led; We who live here, sell spirits and beer; Hoping to get our bread'.

Although religious nonconformity was viewed locally by some with concern, the chapels fulfilled a vital function for Kington Langley beyond offering a venue for divine worship; they provided an outlet for community events and educational opportunities. So that by 1851, a mixed-sex elementary school was established at the Union chapel. During the 1850s, St Peter's church and Langley Fitzurse School were built, financed by local wealthy families and Church of England ministers, to serve the predominantly 'labouring class' population, made up of agricultural labourers and their families. The hope, amongst these elements in the parish, was that the local population would turn away from crime and 'irregularities' (as they saw it), like Sabbath-breaking (such as working or drinking) and that the popularity of nonconformity, which was locally thriving, would be curtailed. In writing a history of

The Jolly Huntsman, Kington St Michael. A public house since 1786 and formerly known as the White Horse.

the parish published in 1858, John Jackson, for example, pointedly referred to there being no resident school at Kington Langley before the creation of the new Church of England-sponsored Fitzurse school. The reason was undoubtedly his disapproval of the school of the Union chapel which was run by nonconformists.

Kington St Michael too continued to have at least one public house throughout the 18th and 19th centuries. The Jolly Huntsman, as the White Horse (it was renamed in the 1970s) on the Street entertained locals according to Britton from 1786, if not before. It later provided a venue for meetings of the local branch of the National Agricultural Union, the St Michael branch of the Ancient Order of Foresters and post-mortem inquests. During the second half of the 19th century, it is likely to have become the main drinking establishment within Kington St Michael, despite possessing only a beerhouse licence until 1931. Meanwhile, at Kington Langley, a beerhouse was established by 1864, which, by 1887, was known as the Hit or Miss.

The sports and cultural life of Kington St Michael burgeoned in the early 20th century. By 1906 the village had a cricket and football team and by 1910 a reading room and village hall. When the primary school was moved to the Ridings in the 1970s the old school and teacher's house became a new village hall. In 2023 regular users of the facilities included Acorns Pre-school and the Women's Institute, and groups from salsa dancing to dog training. A playing field was bought by the parish during the 1980s and in 1997 another community amenity was established, a community woodland, Nymph Hay Wood. Communal amenities were also improved in Kington Langley. A village hall was opened in 1926 on Church Road, funded by donations. It was a popular venue for various social events. A recreation ground was added in the 1960s, and the building was replaced in 1991. In 2023, the village hall was administered by the Kington Langley Village Hall charity and hosted local groups such as the Women's Institute, Film Society, and Croquet Club.

Kington Langley village hall in 1965. Reproduced courtesy of Kington Langley WI

Education provision within the ancient parish of Kington St Michael including Kington Langley was established very early by the nuns at St Mary's priory to girls from wealthy backgrounds entrusted to their care. St Mary's was a Benedictine convent established by 1155, and Aubrey suggested that the girls were likely to have been taught how to read, write and draw alongside surgery and medicine and the art of 'confectionary'. He suggested that in the old hedges around the former lands of the priory were a significant number of berberry-trees which the 'young ladies that were educated there' used in the preparation of confections. It is likely Aubrey was referring to the preparation of sugar-based cures rather than sweets. This education lasted until the priory was dissolved in 1536, after which time the education of girls at least locally lay solely with their families. What education was available to boys is also likely to have been limited or non-existent. It is notable that Aubrey, born in the parish in 1626, learnt to read from John Brome, the Kington parish clerk, but received his first formal education at the hands of Mr Hart, the curate at Yatton Keynell and Robert Latimer, rector, at Leigh Delamere.

Outlined on a plaque in St Michael's church is the gift that created the first village school accessible to all. It was made possible in 1730 by Sarah Bowerman, a widow of St Andrew's, Holborn (Middlesex). Sarah made a bequest in her will that £5 a year be payable forever by the trustees of Christ's Hospital in London, to whom she had gifted property, to pay for a schoolmaster at Kington St Michael for the education of the local poor in reading, writing, accounts and the catechism. It is likely that the school was established the following year and employed a schoolmaster, Daniel Yealf, who, at his death in 1779, had been a schoolmaster in Kington for 48 years. This school was located to the west of the Street near the turning that led to St Michael's church.

Plaque in St Michael's church commemorating the gift of Sarah Bowerman which financed the first parish school accessible to all.

Later, in 1818, ten children attended the school Sarah Bowerman's legacy funded in Kington. The school was also available to children in Kington Langley. In Langley, no other educational provision was noted by the vicar, although it is possible that he chose to ignore any schooling being provided by nonconformist faiths. In Kington there were also three or four dame schools. Unfortunately, over time Sarah Bowerman's gift had been eroded by inflation. John Britton noted c.1825 that the Bowerman-funded school resembled a nursery more than a school, writing, 'what can be done these days for £5 p.a.?' However, it continued, and in

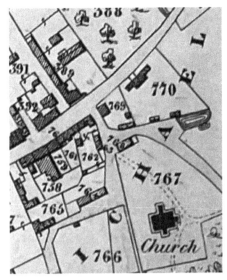

Map dated 1842 showing the outline of the first purpose-built school in Kington at the edge of the churchyard and marked with the number 768. Reproduced courtesy of the Wiltshire and Swindon History Centre, Chippenham, D/1/25/T/A/Kington St. Michael.

1834, charity commissioners reported that the longstanding schoolmaster taught as many children as were sent to him by the minister and churchwardens.

By 1840, a school had been built in Stubbs Lane in Kington at the eastern end of the churchyard. It comprised a single schoolroom with a flagstone floor where 'a one-legged master and a sewing mistress' taught up to 50 boys and girls. A local dame taught 10-15 younger children until they had reached an age to attend the elementary school. It was evident by 1859 that the accommodation at the school in Stubbs Lane was too small. In 1869, a new school and teacher's residence was built on the northern side of the lane leading to the church (subsequently Kington St Michael village hall and shop). The squire, Herbert Prodgers, largely paid for the building himself, which meant that no state funding was needed. The new school, which may have utilised stone from the previous building, accommodated up to 102 pupils.

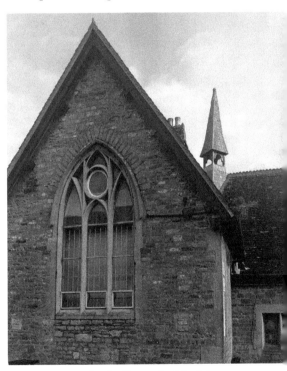

Kington St Michael village school built in 1869, now the village hall and shop.

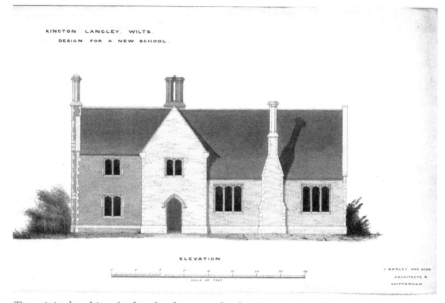

KINGTON LANGLEY, WILTS.
DESIGN FOR A NEW SCHOOL.

ELEVATION

J DARLEY AND SONS
ARCHITECTS &
CHIPPENHAM.

The original architect's plan for the new school at Kington Langley, 1856. Reproduced courtesy of Chippenham Museum, Chippenham, 1985.287.1.

Within a few months of the consecration of a new church in Kington Langley in 1855 planning had begun on a new school. Originally to be called the 'Kington Langley Church of England School', it accommodated 68 pupils and was completed by January 1857. It was later named Langley Fitzurse school.

The new school was built on land donated by Viscount Wellesley of Draycot House. The grant application made to the Lords Committee of Council on Education made explicit the intention to create a school affiliated with the Church of England for the labouring poor, principally children from the families of agricultural labourers. The government subsequently provided a £116 grant, and other grants were made by the National Society for Promoting the Education of the Poor (which was aligned to the Church of England) and the Gloucester and Bristol Diocesan Board. The residue came from wealthy families in the surrounding area. The design outlined in the application included a school room 27 ft. 3 ins. by 16 ft. and a smaller separate classroom. The architects were John Darley and Sons of Chippenham. A planned dwelling for the school master or mistress was not completed until several years later. The classroom space was extended in the late 19th century.

Case Study: In Sickness and in Health: John Jeremiah Daniell's first year as curate of Kington Langley 1858-9

John Jeremiah Daniell the first vicar of St Peter's church, Kington Langley, reproduced courtesy of Wiltshire and Swindon History Centre, Chippenham, 2042/31.

REVEREND DANIELL commenced officiating at St Peter's church Kington Langley in April 1858. He began as a curate, but later became the first parish vicar. Throughout his first ten years in the village, he saw many things which he noted down in a notebook-cum-diary.

The village comprised about 600 souls, but his congregation at St Peter's was often small. Just six came to holy communion at his first Christmas in the parish (although he noted the weather was extremely wet). Congregations were usually largest at Easter and on Ascension day when the school closed early, bolstering numbers with school children. The curate sometimes gave fundraising sermons which were likely to have brought in a bigger congregation. In August Daniell gave a sermon in support of the Church Building Society which raised several pounds; the vicar of Kington St Michael (his church superior) preached in the afternoon of the same day, but only raised a few shillings. Daniell's role drew him into many aspects of village life beyond the walls of St Peter's, and his first year was eventful, punctuated by events great and small, happy and tragic.

Beside the church, Daniell was a regular visitor to the newly opened school. He was closely involved in its organisation. In May the school had its first government inspection. The inspector felt it was 'A very fair building tolerably well supplied with apparatus, but more books and maps are required. The children are decidedly intelligent but have not apparently

St Peter's church, Kington Langley, undated. From the collection of Tim Storer.

been very systematically taught.' Despite the perceived shortcomings the school received a further government grant, and later in the year Daniell noted that the elementary school which had been run at the Union chapel for several years had been closed, presumably as children were moved to the new Church of England school only a few yards away.

A significant celebration recorded each year by Daniell during his time in Kington Langley was the 'school feast'. In 1858, Daniell's first feast began with a church service, presided over by three other clergymen besides himself. Unlike his usual services it attracted a crowd, of 76 children (likely all those who were enrolled at the recently opened Langley Fitzurse school) and about 50 adults. Daniell noted that the congregation included 'several poor'. After the service the children received flags, and accompanied by a cornet playing, the crowd processed to Miss Salter's which was bedecked with flags and a royal banner. The children spent the afternoon enjoying races for marbles, balls and pennies, riding on the swings and chasing 'fire balloons'. Daniell joined in the fun by trying to get an electric shock from a 'galvanic battery' but failed to get a 'severe' jolt. A tea was served (where according to the curate) the children ate too much bread and butter. There was also dancing accompanied by Tom Salter on the violin and afterwards Saul Cole, the village baker, on the bass viol. At 8.30 in the evening the proceedings ended with songs and two renditions of 'God Save the Queen'. Each child left with a piece of cake. The cakes weighing in at a colossal 87lb had been baked by Saul Cole using 8 gallons of dough, 16 lbs of currants, 13 lbs of lard, ½ lb of seeds, 10 lbs sugar, candied peel and numerous eggs.

As idyllic as the school feast sounds, the summer was to turn to tragedy with the death of seven school children in two months from diphtheria, a contagious bacterial infection which affects the nose and throat. Daniell recorded the name of each child in his notebook and officiated at all the burials in the church. The contagion continued into the autumn. Lucy Cole, aged 9, was buried on 30 October, the last of four children in her family to succumb to the affliction in a single month. The last child to die from diphtheria during 1858 was Emma Brind, aged 5. After her funeral service on 9 November, Daniell noted, the mourners sang "There is a happy land" and her classmates threw flowers into her grave.

The school was not just a place of learning, it was a place for communal activities that included readings, possibly organised by Daniell. In early December a crowd of 50 gathered in the school room for a reading and to sing, but on Boxing Day a much less successful reading broke up early after only a few people came to listen and there was 'noisy conduct', probably drunken behaviour, outside. Early in the new year there was a children's concert. Daniell logged the names of all the children who sang but did not record what they sang or how the event was received. However, he noted that two other children were expelled from the school on the same day.

Besides money-raising sermons, Daniell got involved in charitable activities in support of the community, such as by providing supper to the older people at Christmas. Another responsibility was the administration of local charity support to the poor. In September, there was the annual distribution of loaves and alms from Woodruffe's charity. Daniell recorded the names of all those who received loaves of bread and sometimes the reason why the household required support. This included unemployment, and several families where it was necessitated by a large number of children. Two individuals who were blind, Davie Hulbert and Elizabeth Pound also received loaves. A further twelve people each received 6d from the fund. Several people were passed over for alms, possibly a result of Daniell's own intervention, as it caused Elizabeth Hancock, whose husband failed to receive a sixpence, to be 'very saucy' with him. Richard Hancock, likely her son, became an assistant teacher at the school during November. However, perhaps showing the same proclivities as his mother, Richard was 'dismissed for insolence and disobedience' a year later.

The Common, Kington Langley, looking towards the Union chapel and the school, early 20th century. From the collection of Tim Storer.

By the last quarter of the 19th century Sarah Bowerman's annual £5 gift was still being used to help fund the education of children at schools in both villages, but with each passing year the amount was worth less and less. By 1905 the gift was being used simply for a school prize fund.

In 1912, the number of children who could be accommodated in the school at Kington St Michael was reduced to 95, and the following year, the school grounds were extended, both circumstances no doubt reaping benefits to school organisation. Inside the school building, elementary-aged pupils were divided into two classes and taught in the same room, separated by a 5ft screen. Despite the issues which may have been caused by two classes sharing one space, the Board of Education received a good inspection report for classes 1 and 2 in 1922.

School children in front of the lychgate early 1900s. From the collection of Tim Storer.

By 1929, overall school numbers at Kington had dropped to 60, and by 1939, they were as low as 41, although during World War Two they were bolstered with the addition of evacuees, to such an extent that the village hall was being used as school accommodation. In 1956 pupil numbers dropped to 46 when senior pupils (aged 11-15) were transferred to Chippenham Secondary Modern School. The school roll rose and fell through the 1950s and 60s to just 30 in 1969. Numbers recovered during the 1970s, particularly with new housing development locally. In 1975, the head teacher was told that it was not

The new village school opened in Kington St Michael in 1978.

practicable to provide her with an office, and she was offered the use of the cloakroom or kitchen instead. The site was increasingly restrictive, and children had no outside space for organised games. Colonel Showers offered the use of his neighbouring field during the winter, though he asked the children to be careful with the mare and donkey. He later also allowed the use of the field in summer, though it would have to be shared with the cows.

In the mid-1970s the school was described as 'probably the worst school in the north of the county' due to the cramped conditions. In 1976, the Local Education Authority presented the school with a plan for the construction of a new school at the Ridings, at the other end of the village. Problems arose during the building work when contractors went into liquidation. However, approximately 80 pupils were welcomed into the new school on 11 Oct 1978. They were reportedly delighted with the new accommodation, particularly the electric hand dryers and the overhead projector.

In 2023, the voluntarily controlled Kington St Michael Church of England Primary School had 136 children on its roll, drawn from the parish, but also the surrounding villages and housing developments in Chippenham. In addition to the head teacher, it had nine teachers and ten teaching assistants on its books.

At Kington Langley, the LEA raised the prospect of closing the school in 1957. Four years later, proposals were made to build a new school on a different site, opposite the western end of Dovey's Terrace. School managers strongly objected to the proposed site because it was less central than the existing one, and the approach would be via a narrow lane. In 1963 the plan was postponed and after that failed to materialise. Numbers on roll had increased to 100 by 1998, and in the early 2000s a new school hall was built. In 2023, Langley Fitzurse Church of England Primary School was a voluntary-controlled school. It had seven teaching staff and six teaching assistants.

Traditionally the community of Kington St Michael and Kington Langley had looked after their own who had fallen on hard times. Until the mid-17th century this was through charitable giving each Whitsun. Thereafter, occupiers of property paid poor rates, a locally charged tax that was used to provide parish welfare. For older men there was also the Lyte Almshouses in Kington St Michael.

The Lyte Almshouses early 20th century. From the collection of Tim Storer.

Case Study: Lyte Almshouses

ONE OF THE MOST notable buildings of Kington is the row of six almshouses on the village street that bear the inscription, 'Isaac Lyte, Born in this Parish, Alderman of London, Late Deceased, Built this Alms House and indow'd it, Ann Domi 1675'.

The antiquary John Aubrey described Lyte as a 'kinsman' as his great-grandfather was the brother of Isaac Lyte's grandfather. Lyte was also a friend of Aubrey's father. He was not, as has been sometimes said, John Aubrey's grandfather. Isaac Lyte was born at Kington in 1612 and probably apprenticed to a skinner in London where he later became a member of the Skinners Company , one of the great livery companies, and engaged in the fur trade with a business on Broad Street. He was buried in St Mary's Mortlake in Surrey in 1672.

The foundation Lyte established is a source of pride, but it has not always been so. In the early 19th century the antiquary John Britton was not polite about the administration of the almshouses.

opposite page: Tablet and coat of alms on the Lyte Almshouses.

ISAAC LYTE
BORN IN THIS PARISH
ALDERMAN OF LONDON
LATE DECEASED
BUILT THIS ALMS HOUSE
AND INDOW'D
ANN DOMI 1675.

On one occasion, he wrote, 'the almshouses seem to have been in the hand of successive negligent trustees, who have suffered the premises to fall very much into decay. The original institution seems to have been perverted, as the occupation is no longer confined to poor old Batchelors.' Britton was begged by the local squire, Walter Coleman, not to condemn the institution, but he seemingly failed to change Britton's mind.

The origins of the almshouses lay in the bequest made by Lyte in his will dated 1672 for the creation of almshouses in the parish of his birth (spelt 'Keinton'). These he designated for the use of six poor men of the parish. It is possible that building did not begin until after 1707 when (according to notes made for John Britton) property was purchased at Kington and 'the almshouse built on part thereafter, a close containing one acre.' It would also explain why Aubrey, who died in 1697, and a relative of Lyte, did not mention the almshouses in his extensive writings on Kington.

The houses consisted of one building of six tenements. Each initially comprised one room on the ground floor with a bedroom above. To the rear of the building, a half-acre garden was divided into six plots.

On the death of a resident during the mid-late 19th century several candidates were often in contention for the vacant cottage. Each would be proposed and seconded at a vestry meeting (the committee responsible for local government in Kington), and their individual merits debated before one was elected to become an almsperson. The vestry committee also placed rules on the tenants, including restricting their rights to parish poor relief. The role of the vestry meeting is intriguing as, technically, the administration of the almshouses should have been in the hands of six charitable trustees. Whether the intervention of the vestry made the administration of the almshouses more efficient is questionable. In 1862 Thomas Langley and Jack Elms were up for election following the death of an almsperson. Thomas was elected by eight votes to five (a total of 13) to take up the tenancy, but the minutes record that there were only 11 vestry committee members present.

Despite these elections, as Britton's comments suggest, it was not always easy to fill the almshouses with suitable male residents. In 1905, three almshouses were occupied by almspeople, one of whom was a

The Lyte Almshouses early 20th century. From the collection of Tim Storer.

widower, the other two were male but married, and their spouses also lived in the cottage. Another almshouse was rented and occupied by the widow of a former almsperson, and two were unoccupied. A notice had been placed the previous January, but no one had applied for the vacant cottages. By the 1950s almspeople could be single men or women or married couples.

The almshouses were extended to the rear to provide a kitchen, toilet and bathroom by 1962. In the 21st century, alterations were made to each end property to make them appropriate for disabled tenants or couples.

In 2023, the original almshouses and three others were managed by Kington St Michael United Charities (registered charity No. 201283). Trustees were drawn from both Kington St Michael and Kington Langley. The charity also offered allotments to members of the public in the village and the surrounding area in the gardens behind the original building. It is to be hoped under their management the almshouses will be used for many years to come.

Local poor rates were used for centuries to provide welfare to those who needed it most. This relief was organised by annually appointed parish officials called overseers. For the year 1829-30, overseers at Kington (including Kington Langley) provided detailed evidence to a Lords Select Committee, giving us a valuable snapshot of who needed assistance and how their needs were being met. This shows that over a century before the National Health Service was created Kington retained a doctor to provide medical services to the local poor. The parish was also paying for hospital provision. However, their most significant outlay was for the maintenance of the old and infirm. This was largely in the form of cash payments. The next was for widows and single women unable to earn sufficient income, and in these circumstances the parish made up their income to a level deemed sufficient for their maintenance. The parish recognised that even if individuals and families were working their wages might not provide a sufficient income to maintain the household, and consequently Kington had its own scale of benefits based on average weekly wages, the number of children in the household and the cost of bread. In 1829-30, 27 individuals and families had their household income made up in this way and 26 families had their house rents supplemented. This system probably worked well and may have helped to offset the rioting resorted to elsewhere by labourers in the area against low wages.

Unfortunately, in 1834 legislation was passed which overhauled the English welfare system. Henceforth, under this provision Kington residents requiring welfare would only receive assistance by entering Chippenham workhouse. However, there was also the option to apply to local charities or to pay into a friendly society, such as the Wiltshire Friendly Society, which had a branch at Kington from 1857. A friendly society would pay out in the event of illness or accident, and many locally used such schemes to guard against the worst happening.

Besides the Lyte almshouses there were other local charities. At Kington Langley, a short-lived charity called the Clothing Society operated between 1778 and 1808 at Greathouse (Kin House). It was established by Sir James Long of Draycot Cerne with two main objectives: to provide employment for the local poor and to offer free uniforms to domestic servants who were just starting their service, thus eliminating the need to deduct money from their wages.

Other charities had similar objectives. In 1664, William Woodrooff [sic] left 20s. a year to the poor (to be paid to those most in need on 18 September), 'in remembrance' according to his will 'of God's mercy in preserving me in a wonderful manner from drowning at Peckengell Bridge on 18 September 1656.' He also left 10s. to the vicar to preach a sermon on the same day to 'excite and stir up the people to be mindful of mercies returned. And to be in all holy obedience and thankfulness for the same'.

Another 17th-century bequest, by Dorothy Newman, provided an annuity of £6, which was paid to the poor on St Thomas's Day. This was distributed by churchwardens on the advice of the minister among the 'deserving poor', the old and sick, particularly those who attended church regularly and had led blameless lives. By 1834 it had been combined with other bequests to provide bread for the deserving poor on a scale from one to three loaves based on family size.

In the 20th century Buckland's Coal Fund was established by the will of Joseph Whale Buckland which distributed coal to the 20 poorest families of Kington St Michael on Christmas Day. In 1950, while coal was still rationed nationally, £4 was instead distributed among 16 recipients. By 1983 the legacy was still being administered, but the administrator responsible for the distribution informed the minister of Kington St Michael that she knew very little about the fund, what the capital was invested in or the terms of the trust which created it.

Prospect of Kington St Michael church and house sketched by John Aubrey c. 1670. Reproduced courtesy of the Bodleian Libraries, University of Oxford, MSS Aubrey 3, fol 62r.

5
CHURCH, CHAPEL, CONVENT & CLERGY

THE ANCIENT PARISH of Kington St Michael with Kington Langley has had a rich and fascinating religious life. While the church of St Michael dates back to Norman times, prior to the reformation the parish also had chapels at Easton Piercy and at Kington Langley. A new church at Kington Langley was built in 1855. The ancient parish also possessed St Mary's priory, a convent of Benedictine nuns which had its own chapel.

St Mary's priory. 'Restored from a sketch taken by John Aubrey, About A.D. 1660' by Edward Kite c.1858. Reproduced courtesy of the Society of Antiquaries, London, JAC 006.

At Easton Piercy, a small, probably medieval chapel with a graveyard was built adjacent to the manor house on a site northwest of the present manor farm. The chapel was topped with a bell turret in which were mounted two small bells. A very simple building, it was probably something akin to St Giles chapel at nearby Kellaways, that comprised a small square room with two windows and one door, which was demolished in the early 19th century. The only minister recorded for the church at Easton was Ralph de Cromhale in 1319, who was awarded the role by the Lord of Easton manor, John Yeovilton. The structure was pulled down probably at the same time as the new 17th-century manor was constructed, likely providing much of the stone. In the mid-19th century human remains were still occasionally found in the field.

Case Study: St Michael's Church

T HE CHURCH of St Michael's, Kington St Michael has been an integral
part of the parish for centuries, even giving its name to the village. It
has been a place to worship and to pray. But also to celebrate weddings
and baptisms, to meet and decide parish matters. It has been a constant
for almost 1,000 years while the world has changed beyond recognition.
However, at times, St Michael's has been neglected. The control of the
building, its fabric and even its clergy have sometimes caused controversy.

*St Michael's church c.1840. '1st proof' of an engraving made for John Britton,
reproduced courtesy of Wiltshire Museum, Devizes, 1983.4019.*

Although the church was not mentioned in the Domesday book, it
is ancient, and was probably built on the orders of Glastonbury abbey on
a site adjacent to its grange at Kington. The construction of the present

church began in the 1100s, although it has been conjectured that this was
on the site of the older edifice. The structure first comprised a chancel
and nave with a tower to the west. Elements from this time remain and
include the wide arch between the nave and chancel and the columns
beside the door. Originally, the main entrance was on the north side of
the church (not on the south side as it is today) and thus orientated
towards the abbey's grange. In the 17th century John Aubrey made several
sketches of the north doorway, that show a beautiful chevron patterned
arch, the keystone of which was a crowned head. Aubrey believed this to
be King Æthelred. A window, then surviving but now destroyed, in the
south aisle also appeared to show a king and queen which Aubrey also
took to have been a likeness of Æthelred and his queen.

Under the care of Glastonbury abbey, a clergyman was provided
to take services for local people. Relations between the abbey and the
diocese were strained, as the abbey operated independently of the bishop.
In an ensuing power struggle in 1219 and 1275, the control of the church
was, for a time, lost to the bishop. Despite these tumultuous decades, the
structure of Kington parish church was probably remodelled during the
tenure of Michael of Amesbury as abbot of Glastonbury in the period
1235-52. The changes included the addition of a spire to the Norman
tower. The 13th-century chancel with piscina (stone basin) and south aisle
still remain. The south porch was originally added c.1300 from which time
the main entrance lay to the south not to the north.

Ultimately, the abbey lost control of St Michael's church, and from
the late 13th century until the 16th (with some reversions back to the
bishop), it came under the control of St Mary's priory at Kington. Thus,
for the next several hundred years successive prioresses had the choice
of minister at the church, and the priory benefitted from local tithes (a
tax used ostensibly for the support of the church and clergy).

The nuns left their mark on the fabric of the building. This included
windows in the chancel and the addition of a chapel dedicated to the
Virgin Mary, probably at the east end of the south aisle where the
panelled ceiling was painted and gilded. One of the stained-glass windows
was sketched by John Aubrey in the 17th century and depicted the
prioress Christina Nye, who died in 1454. The window was situated at
the east end of the chancel. Another portrait in glass, on the south wall
of the chancel, was of the prioress Celia Bodenham who died in 1511.

John Aubrey's sketch c.1670 showing window (now destroyed) purportedly of King Æthelred. Reproduced courtesy of the Bodleian Libraries, University of Oxford, MSS Aubrey 3, fol 64v.

John Aubrey's sketch c.1670 showing window (now destroyed) of Christina Nye,
prioress of St Mary's who died in 1454, alongside her mother and father. Reproduced
courtesy of the Bodleian Libraries, University of Oxford, MSS Aubrey 3, fol 63r.

Unfortunately, these elements did not survive subsequent restorations of
the church.

Aubrey also made sketches of the exterior of the church that
show its original tower and 13th-century spire topped with a weather
cock. From his anecdotes, we know that the tower contained at least
three bells, one of which was stolen in 1649. The church also had a clock
with iron chimes that struck the hours. During the 'troublesome times',
presumably the civil war period, Aubrey noted that the parish clerk
melted down the chimes for his own use. Prophetically, he also suggested
c.1670 that the tower was in such a poor condition it 'will shortly fall'
and implied that congregants of St Michael's would be to blame as they
were not prepared to pay for its repair. His sketches of the tower show
that it was covered in cracks, and unsurprisingly, it eventually collapsed in
a great storm in 1703. Despite the considerable damage that must have
been sustained to the nave and probably the north aisle, church services
continued to be held in St Michael's for over 20 years before the tower
was eventually replaced. Permission was sought from the diocese to
rebuild the tower minus the spire (doubtless because of the cost), and it
was finally replaced c.1726. Two decades later a new north aisle was also
rebuilt. At this time the Norman entrance on the north side of the church
was destroyed.

The clergy of St Michael's have not been without the stain of scandal. In 1253, the Pope's agent in England was ordered to imprison for life one Walter de Schamel who officiated at the church in Kington. The crime of Walter is unrecorded, but, given the Pope's agent made similar moves against other English churchmen who were accused of forgery around the same time, it may have been for the same crime. Fifteen years later another clergyman, Philip Reyner, who may have ministered at the church, stabbed one William de la Hyde to death at Kington. Richard Hine was vicar for over 50 years in the 17th century. He liked to sing his sermons, and, whether for this reason or another, his congregation were unhappy about his ministry. They complained that he was not 'an able godlye orthodox minister' and paid someone else to take services at St Michael's. Other churchmen have been more orthodox and beloved. Benjamin Griffin was appointed vicar of Kington St Michael in 1712. He died young in 1716 and is commemorated on the north wall of the chancel. Griffin rebuilt the vicarage during his short tenure (a house was provided for the clergyman of St Michael's as early as 1341). Griffin asked to be buried as cheaply as possible and left money to be shared among the local poor. His replacement, William Harrington, also left money to the poor, and he oversaw the building of a new church tower. Harrington's name was memorialised on one of the six church bells.

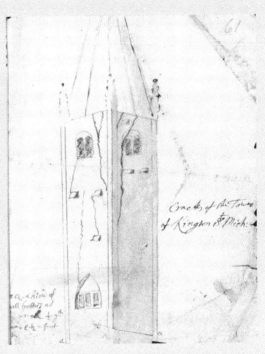

John Aubrey's sketch c.1670 showing the spire of St Michael's church with cracks prior to its collapse in 1703. Reproduced courtesy of the Bodleian Libraries, University of Oxford, MSS Aubrey 3, fol 61r.

Edward Awdry is one of the best-known of the local clergy as vicar of St Michael's from 1856 until 1896. He was a friend of the diarist Francis Kilvert, who was a regular visitor to the parish. However, Awdry's local significance lies in his role in the major renovation of St Michael's and the creation of St Peter's church at Kington Langley.

On being given the vicarage of Kington St Michael, Awdry found the church in a bad state of repair. At first, his parishioners rejected the idea of a restoration, presumably because of the high cost. However, eventually Awdry secured an agreement, and a considerable fundraising effort met the cost. The renovation was extensive. The arches in the nave were strengthened, the roof to the nave and south aisle and several windows were replaced, the vestry to the north of the chancel was rebuilt and the

The plan for the window dedicated to Aubrey and Britton as imagined by Canon John Jackson and the window as completed. John Jackson's sketch reproduced courtesy of Society of Antiquaries, London, JAC 006.

box pews were removed. At the reopening of the church in 1858, Canon John Jackson of Leigh Delamere preached a sermon in celebration, but privately his notes reveal that he felt elements of the renovation went too far. One aspect Jackson fully supported (and may have had a hand in designing) was the new window in the south aisle planned as a memorial to John Britton who died in 1857 and to John Aubrey who died in 1697.

Detail of the infamous east window in the chancel showing Emily Prodgers and children with her hair uncovered.

Several decades later, in 1875 occurred another scandal. The diarist Francis Kilvert recorded that Emily Prodgers, wife of Herbert Prodgers the local squire, and their children had sat for their portraits that would be used in a new window in the chancel. The window was titled 'Suffer little children to come unto me'. Kilvert observed, 'The whole thing is the laughingstock of the village and countryside.' Some parishioners were indignant that Mrs Prodgers should have been the model. According to local tradition, however, the offence was not taken to Mrs Prodgers being portrayed *per se*, but to the fact that she did not have her hair covered. The reaction of Kilvert, himself a clergyman, suggests this may not have been the case as he found her likeness 'not offensive'.

Another local anecdote of Kilvert's was that the people of Kington 'were apt formerly to ring their church bells on the slightest provocation or none at all'. This may, in part at least, have resulted from

Postcard of St Michael's church c.1907. From the collection of Tim Storer.

a local tradition to ring a curfew bell every evening at 8 pm. The tolling of the bell encouraged local people to extinguish lights and fires and to go to bed. This tradition, no doubt dating back to the medieval period, persisted until c.1867 when 'the parishioners grew stingy' and withheld paying 'an old man' whose job it was to ring the bell. In the 20th century St Michael's church hit the headlines when on Christmas day 1990 part of the tower collapsed in high winds during divine service. Mercifully, although four people were injured no one was killed.

By 1171 a place of worship existed in Kington Langley. Religious worship was conducted three times a week at that time, although by 1189 it had fallen into abeyance, and the local congregation was disgruntled. In 1518, the chapel was listed in a manor survey of Glastonbury abbey which recorded that the churchwardens of Langley tenanted the site. The chapel was presumably the same one John Aubrey recorded in 1670 that had been converted into a dwelling. According to Aubrey, the edifice, dedicated to St Peter, stood 'about the middle of the village on the north side of the way'. He provided no description, but it is likely, like the chapel at Easton Piercy, to have been a simple structure. Aubrey did, however, observe that the chapel bell (suggesting a bell turret) had been taken to Fitzurse farm. By this time, the chapel site was part of the Fitzurse estate, and it is likely that the association with Fitzurse was much longer. Indeed, it is possible that the Fitzurse family, who had owned the estate until the 14th century, had traditionally endowed St Peter's chapel. Unlike the chapel at Easton Piercy, St Peter's chapel did not have a graveyard. Instead, corpses were transferred on a trackway, now called Old Coffin Lane, to St Michael's church at Kington.

According to tradition, St Peter's Cottages, on Church Road, occupied the St Peter's chapel site. During the mid-19th century, Canon Jackson observed 'some slight vestiges of which [the chapel] are still pointed out in one of the cottages, not far from the modern little church also called St Peter's.' Jackson sketched one of the vestiges in 1857 but did not give further details. In 1956, the vicar noted, 'A cellar beneath one of the [St Peter's] cottages was apparently a small crypt – but the door of the staircase to it has been bricked up.' According to Historic England, there is no firm evidence of medieval work within the current buildings of St Peter's cottages to support the hypothesis that they were once a chapel. However, It may be that the buildings were entirely rebuilt during the last quarter of the 17th century using the same footprint as the earlier chapel.

St Peter's chapel served the settlement at Langley which was at some distance from the main parish church at Kington. After it became a dwelling, no new church building was built in Kington Langley for one hundred years. Then in the last quarter of the 18th century the squire, Walter Coleman, began work on a new chapel.

Blocked doorway believed to be of St Peter's chapel, Kington Langley, sketched by John Jackson 1857 St Peter's doorway. John Jackson's sketch reproduced courtesy of Society of Antiquaries, London, JAC 006.

Case Study: The Chapel of Walter Coleman

I N KINGTON LANGLEY, on the north side of the Common, just before
its junction with Plough Lane once lay a singular building, a chapel or
mausoleum, whose story appears strange and suffused with betrayal.

The mausoleum was built by Walter Coleman, squire of the village.
Walter was, according to one historian, 'a somewhat eccentric character
even in a family of acknowledged eccentrics.' He was also a 'womaniser'.
Perhaps it was for this reason that he married later in life, aged 57, in May
1778. Elizabeth, his new wife 25 years his junior, had been heavily pregnant
at the time of their nuptials which had been celebrated in France, possibly
to avoid the local glare and gossip.

A few weeks after his marriage, Walter's thoughts seem to have
turned to his death. Whether prompted by illness, the imminent arrival
of his first legitimate child or other reason, Walter conveyed a piece of
land in Kington Langley called 'Batten Patch' to several trustees in order
to erect a 'chapel ... to permit Elizabeth Stephens, the wife of Walter
Coleman, and her children born in his lifetime or wherewith she may be
with child at his decease, and their descendants, to be interred within the
chapel, and any other wife of Walter Coleman or children of him, or any
other persons as he shall direct.'

Walter then stipulated that the chapel could also be used for divine
service or meditation 'by any Society of persons professing Christianity
(except Roman Catholics)' for up to three hours a day. Possibly, Walter
had sympathy with nonconformity, and mention of 'Society' may have
been a reference to the Religious Society of Friends or Quakers, a sect
some of the Coleman family are reputed to have 'professed'. In the
event there is no indication that the chapel was used for divine worship,
although this may seem somewhat surprising given the lack of a church or
chapel in Kington Langley at the time. However, Walter did not register
his chapel or even liaise with the diocese. Given that several vicars came
and went in quick succession and the parish was sometimes without a
churchman for a few months it is possible that Walter's chapel was built
without the bishop's knowledge. The chapel was also a mile or more from
the parish church of St Michael.

Walter died just four years later in May 1782, leaving his wife,
Elizabeth, widowed with two young sons. The chapel was still under

construction at the time of his death, and, perhaps consequently he was first buried in St Michael's church at Kington St Michael. He left a complicated and unusual will that laid out elaborate conditions for the settlement of his estate. But, in his first provision, Walter asked to be 'discreetly and privately' interred in the chapel. He also wanted its construction to be completed. Then outrageously he requested 'the body of Sarah Stephens may be as privately as possible be removed from the parish church yard of Kington St Michael where she is interred and placed in my chapel as near to me as possible'. Later parish registers recorded 'the body [of Walter Coleman] was afterwards removed to a mausoleum built by himself at Kington Langley'. Sarah was the aunt of Walter's widow. It has been speculated that she was a sweetheart from Walter's youth. However, there is no indication another exhumation was carried out or, surprisingly, evidence to suggest that a Sarah Stephens was buried at the Kington churchyard in the first place.

The exact story of the relationship between Elizabeth, Sarah and Walter will never be known, but something could be inferred by the later history of the chapel-cum-mausoleum. It was unfinished on Walter's death, and Walter left a legacy and instructions for its completion. His wishes were not carried out, and the structure was probably never completed. This appears, in large part, to be due to Elizabeth's refusal to pay contractors. There is no mention of the chapel's existence in diocesan recording, such as in notes made by the archdeacon on a visit to the parish in 1787, or by Canon Jackson in a history of the parish published in 1858 when the chapel was still standing. Elizabeth later remarried and neither she nor Walter's sons were interred in the mausoleum. Instead, Elizabeth was buried in St Michael's church at Kington.

No image of the mausoleum has been located, but it appears as a small cruciform 'chapel' on a map of Kington St Michael in 1842. The 'old mausoleum' is mentioned in passing in a diary entry

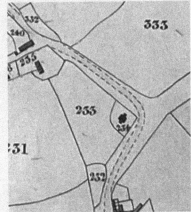

Detail from the Kington St Michael tithe map showing Walter Coleman's chapel near Fitzurse Farm indicated by the number 234. Reproduced courtesy of the Wiltshire and Swindon History Centre, Chippenham, D/1/25/T/A/Kington St. Michael.

of Francis Kilvert, a descendant of Walter's, in 1874, but two years later Kilvert referred to it only as the 'site of the old chapel and burying place where my great-grandfather was laid to rest'.

And so, the mausoleum disappeared from the landscape, and the story from village consciousness. Until in 1931, Robin Tanner married Heather Spackman, and they moved to Kington Langley and built a house. 'As we were wondering what to call the house we noticed that local material arriving for the builders was always addressed "Old Chapel Field." This showed that the official name of the plot on the schedule, Chapel Ground, embodied a still living tradition, so we decided to perpetuate it in the name of the house, though no one could tell us more than we already knew- that one of the old squires had been buried there. A few courses of complete length of wall, from coign to coign, still borders the house on the south side.'

Robin and Heather, whose artistic partnership flourished on the site, assumed that the body of Walter Coleman had been removed from the mausoleum and buried at Kington when the mausoleum fell into disuse. Later, in 1969, Heather examined the parish register, which showed her only that Walter's body had been exhumed from the parish church in 1782, and she conjectured that he could still be under her garden.

Today, the site of the chapel-cum-mausoleum lies under a village garden and its story remains, sadly, something of an enigma.

Etching, The Old Thorn, by Robin Tanner. The stile was at Kington Langley. Reproduced courtesy of Wiltshire Museum, Devizes, 1986.522.

St Peter's church, Kington Langley late 19th century reproduced courtesy of Chippenham Museum, Chippenham, 1978.1273.

Walter Coleman's chapel was never intended to be a parish church. Thus, the churchgoing residents of Kington Langley during the 17th and 18th centuries were, instead, obliged to walk to the main parish church of St Michael at Kington St Michael for services. According to Canon Jackson, who wrote a history of Kington St Michael during the 1850s, this distance 'from clerical superintendence and the wholesome discipline of church and school' eventually produced 'the usual ill effect of ignorance and irreligion' characterised by a rise in crime and 'irregularities of various kinds.' The remedy to these irregularities (by which Jackson also meant the rise in local nonconformity) was to build a new church. This was made a reality through the exertions of Edward

Lewis Clutterbuck of Hardenhuish, and the gift of a site by Walter Coleman's grandson, also called Walter. The new church, dedicated to St Peter, was designed by Charles H. Gabriel of London and Calne and built within a few months. It was consecrated in April 1855.

St Peter's church, Kington Langley, early 20th century, from the collection of Tim Storer.

The clergy of St Michael's church, who historically also officiated at Kington Langley until 1865, have been an essential part of the community for centuries. The first named clergyman is William St Faith c.1173 about whom we know little. The tenure of Jordan Cotel as the rector of Kington in the 13th century was troubled due to a strained relationship with the abbot of Glastonbury, who owned most of the parish. The abbot deprived Cotel of pasture to graze his cattle, obstructed a road, and built houses at Kington Langley, all to Cotel's annoyance. An agreement was finally made in 1269 whereby Cotel released the abbot from all damages and renounced some of his rights to graze livestock. In return, he retained some rights to run pigs and graze his cattle with those of the abbot and had the right to use local roads.

From the late 13th century, the prioress of St Mary's priory chose who was made vicar of the parish church. In 1387, the prioress chose Roger Knyght to take the post. Five years later, Knyght was suspended from the vicarage after he confessed to the bishop he had grave faults. It is not recorded what these flaws were, but at the time, clergymen were occasionally sent to the convent as penance for sexual immorality. If Knyght's faults lay in this direction, he would have been given short shrift.

Richard Hine became vicar of Kington St Michael in 1612. A graduate of Oxford University, he held the post for over 50 years through the Civil War and interregnum. By 1650, Hine's parishioners were so frustrated with him that services were being taken by Nicholas Peirce, who received £15 from the vicar's income, the rest continuing to be paid to Hine. The congregation did not manage to get rid of Hine until he died in 1663. On his death, Hine left bequests to his seven children and sixteen grandchildren. His most valuable asset was his books. He was interred in the churchyard at St Michael's alongside his wife, Anne, who, according to Aubrey, was a midwife who told fantastic tales.

Edmund Garden was vicar from 1779 until his death at 92 in 1824. Like many before him, Garden held other posts within the Church of England, including one at the church of St Botolph without at Aldgate in London. He was also chaplain (or chapel reader) at Gray's Inn, London. According to the archdeacon in 1787, Garden only lived in Kington for two or three months a year, during the summer months, presumably when London became uncomfortable. During his long absences, services were taken by a curate, John Kemble, who lived in the vicarage. According to Garden's obituary, 'he was a man of the most benevolent disposition, and his long life was passed in the practice of every Christian virtue'. His passing does not seem to have been particularly mourned in Kington parish, probably because they saw little of their vicar's attention or 'Christian virtue.'

Edward Awdry, a friend of the diarist Francis Kilvert who often visited the parish, was vicar from 1856 until 1896. Kilvert sometimes preached at St Michael's and knew the village well. Awdry made a significant impact during his tenure, which included the major renovation of St Michael's church and the creation of St Peter's church at Kington Langley. His obituary stated, 'No priest was ever held in greater reverence, love and esteem by his flock, than Mr Awdry whose kindly, generous and courteous disposition will long be cherished by his old parishioners'.

A late 19th century photograph of the chancel of St Michael's church much as Francis Kilvert would have known it. Reproduced courtesy of the Society of Antiquaries, London, JAC 006

At first services were taken in the new church of St Peter's by curates from Kington St Michael, but in 1865 Kington Langley (as Langley Fitzurse) was made an ecclesiastical parish with its own curate, John Jeremiah Daniell. Daniell was an accomplished writer whose works included histories of Chippenham and Warminster. During his tenure at St Peter's Daniell kept a diary in which he recorded anecdotes about the life of St Peter's and the village community between 1858 and 1868 (see above, pages 109-12).

Case Study: St Mary's Priory

St Mary's priory c.1670 sketch made by John Aubrey. Reproduced courtesy of the Bodleian Libraries, University of Oxford, MSS Aubrey 3, fol 67r.

A S THIS BOOK demonstrates, the ancient parish of Kington St. Michael is singular. One of the most compelling reasons is that it was the site of a Benedictine convent.

St Mary's priory existed at Kington St Michael by 1155 but may have been founded before that date. The earliest known written evidence for St Mary's priory dates from when Joselin was bishop of Old Sarum between 1142 and 1155. At this time, Robert Wayfer (of Brimpton, Berkshire) gave gifts to the 'nuns of Kington' necessary to create a new priory. According to John Aubrey, local people believed Empress Matilda (1102-1167) had founded the house. However, as the nuns remembered Robert, and not Matilda, each year it is likely that Robert was also responsible for the foundation of St Mary's priory. Robert was a layman and not a nobleman. It is probable that in providing for the nuns he was supporting women from his own family – possibly Emma, the sister of his wife, Eva, who are both named on his grants to the nuns. Emma became a nun at Kington yet surprisingly is not named as the prioress.

Robert was the first recorded benefactor of the convent but by no means the last. Others included the Bishop of Bath & Wells. Another patron was Petronilla Bluet. Petronilla was a remarkable woman. As a child (as young as 7), she was married to the aged Dermod McCarthy (or Diarmit mac Carrthaig), King of Cork in Ireland. Dermod's marriage to Petronilla, a noble Anglo-Norman woman, helped cement his submission to Henry II, but also led to his assassination in 1185. Petronilla later married again, to William de Felcham and gave land at Bradley, Hampshire, in her own right to the priory between 1194 and 1199.

The priory of Kington was never rich, but it contained riches. These included a bone of St Christopher kept in a cloth of gold, possibly the only saint's relic held by the priory. There were also the books, including a copy of the saints' lives in English and a book of matins. Both would probably have been beautifully illuminated. However, the glory of the convent was the 'very fayre' chapel of St Mary's. Constructed by 1185, it was considerably refurbished in the early 15th century. Of significance was the statue of the Saviour in the chapel, and images of both St Michael (possibly from the association with the parish church) and another of St Katherine (likely depicted with the wheel on which she was supposedly crucified) looking resplendent in St James' chapel, perhaps a chantry chapel to the eastern part of the church. There were also 'three yards' of canvases (presumably depicting the life of St James the apostle) on the altar. The surviving west range of the priory (now manor) dates from the early 15th century. We know that the income of the priory was never significant but it did not accrue large debts. So the high quality construction of the remaining priory range and the fine improvements to the chapel (we have sketches made before its destruction) suggest that the convent must have had a generous benefactor. A possibility is Cardinal Henry Beaufort (1374-1447), step-brother to Henry IV, a lavish supporter of church causes, whose life was annually remembered by the nuns.

St Katherine, the image that adorned St James' chapel, was the patron saint of young girls, students and craftsmen who worked with wheels. She had particular significance to the convent. The convent was a house of God but also a place of learning. According to Aubrey, the girls were taught to write and draw, and to practice physic and surgery to heal the sick and injured. A skill, he lamented, that was no longer taught to young women. The girls were also trained in 'needlecraft' and the art of making confectionery. 'This' he wrote 'was a fine way of breeding up young women, who are led more by example than precept: and a good retirement for widows and grave single-women to a civil virtuous and holy life.' The good retirement for widows and grave women Aubrey mentioned was not the life of nuns, but vowesses, women who had made a vow of chastity and refused (re)marriage. These women could retain land and property and the liberty to travel beyond the cloister. However, they were linked to it. It supported them spiritually and practically, and in turn, they supported the house. One of these women may have been Petronilla Bluet, widow of Dermod, King of Cork. Alongside the nuns and vowesses were the two king's almswomen, whose maintenance was paid not by their gifts to the priory but by the crown. A house was built for them in 1221, which was probably timber-framed and thatched.

St Mary's priory in 1795. Sketch by John Jackson from an original by John Britton. Reproduced courtesy of the Society of Antiquaries, London, JAC 006.

Although the religious life gave women a freedom, of sorts, the priory still needed men. The most important was the priest who lived within the house (his chamber was to the right of the porch) to officiate at religious services. In 1536 the women also had a steward, responsible for collecting money owed to the priory and overseeing workers (of which there were four) on the home farm. There was also the clerk and a male waiting servant. During earlier centuries, there may have been more male retainers. There were also four female servants (when there were only four nuns). Men were also sent on pilgrimage to the priory to do penance for their sexual transgressions. In 1394, one such was Thomas, a bailiff who committed adultery with Margaret, a woman whom he kept as a mistress in Salisbury. Another from the same year was an unnamed

chaplain who had fornicated with Julianna of Ham. Both men had to pay
the prioress 20s.

Although the nuns enjoyed independence within the priory, they
were subject to supervision by the local bishop and this caused some
problems for the house. In 1490 the prioress Alice Lawrence sought to
rid the priory of the intrusion by instructing a Franciscan friar to forge
a letter from the pope to the abbot of Glastonbury. The falsified letter
instructed the abbot, Richard Whiting, that the supervision of the nuns at
Kington had been moved from the diocese to his care. The letter included
complaints that the bishop had visited the convent 'as often as he like(d)'
with retinues of secular attendants who appropriated accommodation
from the nuns and required expenses which the convent could ill afford.
It is telling that the letter also suggested that under the new arrangement
the prioress and convent would 'be able to serve God more securely
and quietly, and the frequent offences that arise out of its subjection to
secular persons will in future be avoided.' It may be that the women were
placed in danger by the men who were visiting them. The abbot was part
of the same Benedictine order as the nuns and a local landowner, so
perhaps Alice Lawrence and the abbot were on good terms. The bishop
was, however, suspicious and wrote to the pope, and the ruse was soon
detected. Alice resigned.

The yearly net income of St Mary's was just £25 when the priory
was dissolved in 1536 (compared with £601 for Wilton abbey or £495 for
Amesbury abbey, the other Benedictine foundations of nuns in the county,
or £168 for the canonesses of Lacock abbey, the only other nunnery in
Wiltshire). Yet the estate was locally economically and socially significant.
The priory had orchards, gardens, two mills (one powered by horse) and
a dovecot. The farm included:

196 acres of arable land.

34 acres of pasture and meadow.

Rights to graze animals in Heywood.

Land in the parish was worked by their servants or rented out. Money
and goods flowed into the parish from the property, and from the tithes
that the nuns received from elsewhere, including Petronilla's property
in Hampshire, owned by the nuns centuries after her death. Kington's
weekly market at the cross (the junction of Honey Knob Hill and Grove
Lane) was held chiefly (so Aubrey thought) for the benefit of the convent.

From the late 13th century the nuns also chose the minister of St
Michael's church and were responsible for the upkeep and improvement
of its chancel (including some stained glass). The nuns ministered to the
local sick and gave alms. Women joined the convent as nuns or vowesses,
some from many miles away. The priory attracted visitors and travellers
to Kington who brought money, goods, news and excitement from the
wider world. Not all were welcome, since in 1511 the curate of Castle
Combe, Thomas Kelley, 'robbyd the pore monastery of Kyngton, and
caryd away the prioresse.' Kelley was a noted womaniser. We do not
know if the prioress was compliant. However, she never returned.

The Priory at KINGTON ST MICHAEL, WILTS.

*St Mary's priory 1803. Sketch by John Britton printed in the
Gentleman's Magazine.*

All ended at the reformation when Henry VIII broke with the catholic church. The priory was dissolved in 1536 when only four nuns remained. The last prioress, Marye Dennis, was given a small pension. She lived until 1593, by which time the priory and its estate had been sold several times, and the buildings were gradually falling into decay. The graves of the nuns were regularly being dug up by the time of John Aubrey in the mid-17th century and 'in the chappell which was very fayre, is neither glasse, chancel nor monument remayning'. By 1803, John Britton described how one side of the original quadrangle had been taken down and the remaining two had been so much altered that very little remained. The 'ancient hall' was used as a kitchen, while the kitchen garden occupied the former graveyard. An archway that belonged to the chapel was still standing, but the site of the chapel was in use for pig sties. A sad end to a beautiful and much-loved place.

St Mary's priory, early 20th century. From the collection of Tim Storer.

Photograph showing Kington St Michael vicarage in 1906. From the collection of Tim Storer.

The vicar of Kington St Michael was provided with a house as early as 1341, if not before. From the 16th century this residence lay to the south-west of the church on the south side of Stubbs Lane. In 1663, during the tenure of John Ferris as vicar of Kington St Michael, the simple accommodation comprised parlour chamber, parlour, malt loft, buttery, kitchen and a chamber over the parlour and another over the buttery. Ferris's household was quite self-sufficient. The vicar had c.18 a. of pasture and arable land and kept pigs, although he probably employed staff to farm the land and tend animals on his behalf. The household was also brewing beer and making cheese and butter. The house and lands of the vicar were called the glebe, while the glebe provided some (traditionally one-third) of Ferris's approx. £60 annual income, more was made up by tithes. By 1889, the vicar, Edward Awdry, enjoyed an income of £350 per annum gross from the tithe rent charge (from the 1840s parishioners no longer paid the vicar in produce but a charge on the land they occupied). Awdry earned just c.£36 from renting out the glebe lands.

The vicarage was remodelled c.1712-16 when Benjamin Griffin was vicar. It was altered again in the 19th century. The house is now called the Old Rectory and is grade II listed.

In 1676, 331 adults worshipped at St Michael's church. In 1851, numbers remained high, and the average number of communicants was recorded as 260 in the morning and 330 in the afternoon, including 70 Sunday Scholars at both services. Despite these figures, not everyone in Kington St Michael or Kington Langley was happy to worship at St Michael's church. From the 17th century protestant dissenting or nonconformist sects drew some away from the Church of England.

By the 1670s there was an active Quaker community in Kington St Michael and Kington Langley (up to an estimated 30 in 1676). Quaker teachings emphasised a direct relationship with God, rejected creeds, clergymen and set forms of worship, something which set them against the doctrine of the Church of England. Quakers were often met with hostility and fear. They were persecuted, most often given fines for their non-attendance at church or failure to pay tithes which at the time were obligatory. Prosecutions were often initiated by Church of England ministers.

An 18th-century Quaker meeting listening to an eminent preacher, Benjamin Lay.

In 1672 the Quaker, John Gingell who lived at the former priory of St Mary at Kington, was prosecuted for the non-payment of tithes, following a complaint by the vicar, John Ferris. Ferris's income was partially dependent on tithes. It may have been understandable, therefore, that Ferris was somewhat exasperated. However, according to the *Wiltshire Friends Suffering Book*, a volume kept by the county's Quakers to record their maltreatment, Gingell was sued after refusing to pay 30s., after which Ferris 'had taken from him one horse worth £6'. £6, a large amount of money at the time, was worth 120 shillings, four times the amount John owed. It may have rankled Ferris that John Gingell's family was an old and respected one within the parish. Despite John's treatment, his Quaker faith remained strong and he was later imprisoned for four months in 1684 for refusing to worship at the parish church. During the same year, seemingly in defiance, his home was used as a Quaker meeting house. The old priory was probably convenient as it was close to the village, but far enough away to avoid constant oversight. However, the vicar and churchwardens were determined. In the same year, one of the churchwardens of Kington, Thomas Stoaks (Stokes?), appears to have organised the imprisonment of Quakers (including another Kington resident, Charles Barrett senior) at a house in Sutton Benger while he went to get a warrant for their arrest. On the following day Stoaks 'carried them' before Justice Talbot. The Quakers, including Charles Barrett, were committed to prison for three months for refusing to swear an oath of allegiance to the Church of England. If the vicar and churchwardens hoped to have put people off becoming Quakers, they were to be disappointed. In 1686, Kington churchwardens presented the bishop with a long list of people who did not receive holy communion.

After the enactment of the Act of Toleration in 1689, Quaker worship was allowed, within constraints. and a Charles Barrett (possibly the son of Charles Barrett senior) had his dwelling in Kington registered as a Quaker meeting house. Despite, the relaxation of the rules on their worship, the persecution of local Quakers continued into the 18th century. Notably, the Quaker preacher Roger Cook, who lived in Kington, had goods confiscated annually from 1707 until his death in 1718 for the non-payment of tithes, something Quakers were still expected to pay. Sometime later, in 1742 at Kington Langley a, likely Quaker, meeting house was registered at the home and barn of Richard Dovey. Despite this, the popularity of Quakerism locally was on the wane and by the end of the 18th century the vicar reckoned there were no nonconformists in either Kington St Michael or Kington Langley. However, in the 19th century religious nonconformity once again developed rapidly.

The Common, Kington Langley with the Union chapel and St Peter's church in the distance, early 20th century. From the collection of Tim Storer.

In Kington Langley, in 1823, Wesleyan meetings were recorded at the dwelling of John Gough, a local labourer. Later, in 1834, a house occupied by James Piniger (likely Pinnegar) in Kington St Michael (most probably at Kington Langley) was registered as a chapel. The following year the newly constructed Union chapel, built by J. Pinnegar, James Pinnegar a local mason, was registered on Middle Common in Kington Langley. The chapel was built by subscriptions. It was vested in trust for use by Moravian, Baptists and Independent denominations. It was noted on its opening that the chapel was the only place of worship for two miles. The chapel was popular and filled to capacity for Sunday worship to the annoyance of the local Church of England clergy.

In 1843/4 another chapel was built in Kington Langley; this one was located on Silver Street and used by Primitive Methodists. Like the Union chapel it was immediately popular. Reportedly rebuilt in 1878, during the 1920s the number of worshipers at the chapel was said to be in excess of that of St Peter's church and Union chapel combined. Later, however, the number of congregants diminished, and in 1987 the chapel was closed and converted for domestic use. The independent Bethesda chapel was erected in 1835 in Kington St Michael. The chapel, like the Union chapel, was in shared ownership and administered by local trustees. These included the minister Benjamin Rees and George Tanner, a local mason. By 1851, 70 congregants were attending worship at the chapel. However, like the chapel on Silver Street its popularity waned in the 20th century and by 1985 it had been closed and converted to a dwelling.

Bibliography and Additional Notes

This book is based on research carried out by Mark Forrest and me for the Wiltshire Victoria County History (VCH) volume 20 on Chippenham and the surrounding area. It makes extensive use of primary source material from a number of archives and online repositories. As with any place-based history, there were sources that were not examined and further lines of enquiry that could be pursued. Below, I have noted some, not all, of the sources that were looked at but which may provide a starting point for further investigation.

The earliest documentary evidence for the Kingtons are the Anglo-Saxon charters from 934 (S.426), 940 (S.473) and 987 (S.866). However, these and the later Domesday survey contain somewhat confusing and conflicting information about the area now identified as the parishes of Kington St Michael and Kington Langley. A useful discussion is made in the parish histories of Kington St Michael and Kington Langley that will be published in Wiltshire VCH vol. 20.

Some of the most important medieval sources for the villages are those created by Glastonbury abbey who owned much of the ancient parish of Kington St Michael which at that time included Kington Langley. Many of these are lodged at Longleat House, Warminster. For example, the detail on the terrible outcome of the Black Death in chapter 2 was possible through examination of manuscript MS 11179. An important survey was conducted by Glastonbury abbey on the manor of Kington St Michael in 1189. This was published in the original Latin by Canon John Jackson in his volume *Liber Henrici De Soliaco Abbatis Glaston* in 1882. See also N.E. Stacy (ed.), *Surveys of the estates of Glastonbury Abbey. c.1135-1201* (2001). Another survey of the manor was made in 1518 and is located in the British Library (Harl. Ms. 3961).

A detailed history of the ancient parish from earliest times, also by John Jackson, was published in *Wiltshire Archaeological and Natural History Magazine* vol. 3, in 1858. In it Jackson reproduced transcriptions of some early documents including the calendar of obits for St Mary's priory created in 1493 – a list of benefactors, brethren and nuns, whose names were mentioned in the prayers of the convent upon the 'days of their respective deaths'. Jackson's extensive notes, photographs, drawings, clippings and more which he used in the creation of this account of the Kingtons (and which he continued to maintain for decades afterwards) can be found at the Society of Antiquaries of London (JAC 006).

Extensive use was made of the manuscript and published works of John Aubrey (1626-1697). The principal manuscript repository for Aubrey's work is the Bodleian Library in Oxford. MS Aubrey 3 (fol 55r-80v) encompasses Aubrey's notes on Easton Piercy (Easton Piers), Kington St Michael and Kington Langley (Langleigh) which he collected to form part of a topographical history of Wiltshire that was never completed. This manuscript was later edited, 'corrected' and enlarged by Jackson and published in 1862. The sections on Kington St Michael and Kington Langley and Easton Piercy are invaluable in making Aubrey's text more organised and readable, but Jackson's editing and manipulation of the text is also problematic. Some of the problems are highlighted below. Aubrey's *Natural History of Wiltshire* (MSS Aubrey 1 and 2) also refer to Kington St Michael. A version of this manuscript (MS/92) was given by Aubrey to the Royal Society in London where it remains to this day. An edited text based on this version was published by John Britton in 1847. In the illustrations for this volume, I have used another of Aubrey's manuscripts at the Bodleian, MS Aubrey 17, *Designatio de Easton-Piers in Com: Wilts*, a series of coloured views of Easton Piercy.

Like John Aubrey, the antiquary John Britton was born in Kington St Michael. Britton's autobiography, published in 1850, includes important anecdotes of his early life in Kington during the late 18th century. Britton planned to write a history of Kington and while this was never published, many of the materials he collected are in Wiltshire Museum, Devizes along with many other papers on Wiltshire history more broadly. Those I have used extensively include MSS 107 and 4080, an unpublished manuscript entitled 'Topographical Collections for the Hundreds of Chippenham and North Damerham, County of Wilts'. I have also used Britton's book *Memoir of John Aubrey FRS*, published in 1845 and *The Beauties of Wiltshire: Displayed in Statistical, Historical and Descriptive Sketches*, vol. 3, from 1825.

Other Wiltshire Museum manuscripts utilised are MSS 807/1-2, a collection of notes on the families and history of Kington St Michael, with pedigrees, details of land tenure, and extracts from Court Rolls, and the 18th-century notebook of James Gilpin, MSS 4019, which includes notes transcribed from Aubrey's manuscripts. The museum also houses a wonderful collection of artworks and archaeological artefacts, including etchings by Kington Langley resident Robin Tanner.

The Wiltshire and Swindon History Centre (WSHC) in Chippenham was the principal repository of primary sources (abbreviated WSA) employed in the research for this book. These sources are numerous and include deeds, accounts, minutes and more. Amongst those used in the research for several chapters are the manor court book 1558-1588 (WSA, CC/Bish/459/1); the 1655 manor survey (WSA, 873/140) and the tithe map for the Kingtons created in 1842 (WSA, D/1/25/T/A/Kington St. Michael). There is also an abundance of documents on schools in Kington Langley (references begin WSA, F8/600/166/) and Kington St Michael (starting WSA, F8/500/157/). These include school logbooks, managers logbooks, minutes, deeds and more. Other surviving sources are not as complete. For example, WSHC hold no vestry minutes for Kington St Michael before 1854 and no overseers' or highway surveyors' accounts and no churchwardens' accounts prior to the 20th century.

The resources of the National Archives (TNA) at Kew were also exploited. The TNA hold a number of local wills that were proved (authorised) at the Prerogative Court of Canterbury. These are currently (2024) available for free download. Examples include the extraordinary will of Walter Coleman (TNA, PROB 11/1090/204) from 1782 referenced in the case study on his chapel in chapter 5 and the will of Isaac Lyte (TNA, PROB 11/342/531) which established the Lyte almshouses at Kington St Michael mentioned in the case study in chapter 4. Also available for download are the returns for census Sunday 1851 (TNA, HO 253/129) which provide a snapshot of local religious life in the early Victorian period. Returns for the Kingtons are grouped together with a number of other parishes. Unfortunately, other sources require a visit to the TNA. Amongst these are the local school files (e.g. TNA, ED 21/18455 for Kington St Michael 1872-1913 and TNA, ED 21/18454 for Langley Fitzurse 1872-1912) and the MAF (agricultural) returns (e.g. TNA, MAF/68/73 (Kington St Michael 1866)).

The Kington Langley vicar, John Jeremiah Daniell, kept a diary between 1858 and 1868. Various versions of this exist, including one at WSHC (WSA, 2042/1) and one at Wiltshire Museum (MSS 1845). Another was published in a history of Kington Langley written by its later vicar Canon W J Meers (*Historical Notes on Two Villages in Wiltshire: Langley Fitzurse and Draycott Cerne* (revised and enlarged, 1956)). Meers's book also provides a helpful introduction to the history of Kington Langley. The diaries of the Victorian churchman Francis Kilvert, who lived at nearby Langley Burrell, were also used extensively in the research for this book. This text provides valuable insight into local life during the 1870s. There are a number of published versions available.

Aside from the secondary sources already referenced, the books of June Badeni *Past People in Wiltshire and Gloucestershire* (1992) and *Wiltshire Forefathers* (1982) proved helpful. However, the single most referenced book in the VCH history of the Kingtons is *Wiltshire: the Topographical Collections of John Aubrey* (1862). This is a volume of Aubrey's topographical manuscript creatively edited and enlarged by John Jackson referred to earlier. Extensive use was made of the Wiltshire Record Series (WRS) volumes, 76 in number and counting. These books provide transcribed and organised versions of original documents. Amongst those examined were volumes 27 (*Wilts. Returns to the Bishop's Visitation Queries 1783*); 40 (*Wilts. Dissenters Meeting House Certificates*) and 56 (*Wilts. Glebe Terriers*). Also valuable were the eight volumes of the *Wiltshire Notes and Queries*, and issues of the *Wiltshire Archaeological and Natural History Magazine*, often known as WAM. Many WRS and WAM volumes can be found online. However, these volumes and all the books noted here are available at WSHC, which I recommend to anyone interested in Wiltshire history. Also available at WSHC are trade directories, a must for any local historian, and especially useful for the period from the 1850s to the early 20th century. Furthermore, the centre has a selection of government reports dealing with charities, schools and welfare and numerous volumes on all aspects of Wiltshire history. Pre-eminent among the latter are the volumes of the Wiltshire Victoria County History, particularly Volume 3 which covers the religious history of Wiltshire, including an account of St Mary's priory at Kington St Michael, and Volume 4 that contains essays on the agricultural and industrial history of the county and information on aspects of tax and population.

Research for this volume made extensive use of online databases and websites. I have not included specific URLs as websites may change, but they should be easily found through a web search. Some online repositories, such as the British Newspaper Archives (BNA) and Ancestry, require a subscription. The BNA provides access to many Wiltshire papers particularly from the early 19th century to the early 20th century, such as the *Wiltshire Times* and *Trowbridge Advertiser* and *Devizes and Wilts. Gazette*. Ancestry was invaluable in providing access to parish registers and local wills and probate documents. Databases not requiring a subscription include the Clergy of the C of E Database (for details about post-reformation clergy); Electronic Sawyer (for the text of Anglo-Saxon charters) and Wilts. Historic Environment Record (which provides information on the county's archaeology and historic built environment). The websites used included that of Historic England, for information about listed buildings, and Know Your Place: Wiltshire, from where were accessed old editions of Ordnance Survey maps as well as the tithe map of the villages. These were particularly useful in the preparation of chapter 1.

There are a few aspects I wish to highlight about specific chapters. In chapters 1 and 5, I suggested that the chapel at Easton Piercy was demolished c.1631. In his writings , Jackson proposes two alternative dates: 1610 (WAM, 4 (1858), 73) and 1640 (Aubrey, *Topog. Colln.* ed. Jackson, 236). In fact, Aubrey states the date was 40 years before his time of writing (probably 1671, according to the catalogue at the Bodleian Library for Aubrey's Wiltshire notes, MSS Aubrey 3) and thus 1631, the same as the datestone on the new manor house at Easton Piercy. The two events are probably, therefore, linked, which led me to suggest that the stone from the chapel was reused in the new house. On the topic of Aubrey, it is worth pointing out that in the 17th century the new year began in March, so Aubrey refers to his date of birth as March 1625 and not March 1626, which has caused confusion in the past.

Also in chapter 1 while I say that there is no image of Langley Fitzurse manor, there is one exception, the photographs of its barn which survive from the 20th century, one of which is reproduced at the beginning of the Langley Fitzurse case study.

The case studies on wartime in chapter 3 relied on a wide range of sources. They included books. Amongst those used were *From Old Chapel Field: Selected Letters of Robin Tanner* (1991); *Out of Nazi Germany* by Heather Tanner and

Dietrich Hanff published in 1995, and the wonderful *Blackouts to Bungalows* by Julie Davies from 2016. Much of the detail was only possible through a close examination of local newspapers through the war; finds included the *Wiltshire Times and Trowbridge Advertiser* from 23 June 1945 which reported on the wartime activities of Westinghouse at Kington Langley. Other significant sources include school logbooks and managers' minutes (such as for Kington St Michael WSA, F8/600/157/1/3/1 and F8/500/157/1/1), parish council minutes (for Kington St Michael, WSA, 1787/1/1) and the parish war book (WSA, F2/851/4) which has unfortunately only survived for Kington St Michael. At the TNA are the wartime MAF reports (Kington Langley TNA, MAF 32/39/33 and for Kington St Michael TNA, 32/39/34). This chapter also features the 1822 Langley revel. This was described in numerous press reports from across the region, including *Devizes and Wiltshire Gazette,* 12 September 1822; *Morning Post* 13 September 1822 and *Taunton Courier,* 18 September 1822.

For chapter 4, I want to draw attention to the wills of Isaac Lyte (TNA, PROB 11/342/531), which established the almshouses and that of Sarah Bowerman (TNA, PROB 11/641/342), that created the first local school accessible to all. The strange affair of the 1900 near-riot at Kington St Michael was well reported in newspapers. The reports which were used included *Wiltshire Times & Trowbridge Advertiser* 10 March 1900; *Chard & Ilchester News* 10 March 1900, *Southern Times & Dorset Herald*, *Bristol Mercury* 7 March 1900 and the *Devizes & Wiltshire Advertiser* 8 March 1900. Chapter 4 also features a case study on local superstition and folklore. Much of this is drawn from the writings of John Aubrey; indeed, tales of folklore and superstition pepper Aubrey's work, while other works specifically address the topic. These include *Remaines of Gentilisme and Judaisme and Miscellanies,* the only book he published in his lifetime.

In chapter 5, I propose that by the 17th century, the original chapel of St Peter at Kington Langley had been part of the Fitzurse estate. This is because the land appears as part of Bampfield Sydenham's (d.1697) Fitzurse estate. It was later occupied by Walter Coleman who gifted the site for the creation of the new church (WSA, 873/132). Information about the closure and conversion of the Primitive Methodist chapel was provided by David Martin Mullis in March 2023. Tim Couzens gave information about local Quakers.

I never cease to be moved by the courage of local Quakers in the face of persecution and would encourage anyone with an interest to take a look at the Wiltshire Friends Sufferings Book (WSA, 1699/18) at WSHC in which local Quakers lay out how they were locally persecuted in the period 1653-1756. Although this has an obvious bias.

John Jackson's editing of Aubrey's topographical work caused me a few problems in the case study on St Michael's church at Kington St Michael. In his published version of Aubrey's notes, Jackson tried to edit out some inconsistencies in Aubrey's account. For example, Jackson shows a representation of what he says is taken from Aubrey's sketch of the south door of St Michael's church at Kington St Michael (Aubrey, *Topog. Colln*. ed. Jackson, 134). This sketch in *Architectura Chronologica* is actually of the north door. This is confirmed by another sketch Aubrey made of the north door in the margins of his topographical manuscript (Bodleian Library, MS Aubrey 3 fol. 66r). In misrepresenting Aubrey›s sketches Jackson was trying to resolve an error made by Aubrey in his topographical text and the evidence as Jackson saw it provided by the south door of St Michael›s. According to Historic England (HER 1283509), the south door of St Michael›s has Norman shafts, and the door and door head are 15th or 16th century, again confirming that the Norman doorway sketched by Aubrey must have been the north door.

In the piece on the chapel of Walter Coleman the text of the conveyance is taken from a transcription of the document made by Heather Tanner and reproduced by the Kilvert Society in their March Newsletter in 1969 (see also June 1967, Sep 1969). I have not located the original. I state that there is no indication that Sarah Stephens was exhumed from the graveyard at St Michael's at Kington St Michael based on the parish registers and diocesan records. However, notes set down in 1913 by W T Coleman (probably Walter Thomlinson Coleman, Walter's direct descendant) in Wiltshire Museum (MSS 807/2) record 'after his interment, by the direction of his will, the body of Mrs Sarah Stephens the Aunt of Elizabeth his wife was privately removed from Kington Churchyard where she was interred and placed by his side in a grave made for that purpose in the Chapel.' W T Coleman called Sarah 'Mrs' Sarah Stephens. Stephens was Sarah's birth name, and presumably, as Walter Coleman referred to her as 'Sarah Stephens', she had not married. It is possible that W T Coleman was using 'Mrs' as an abbreviation for 'Mistress', a title used for an educated or higher-status woman. How much faith to give W T Coleman is difficult without further corroborating evidence.

Index

This is an index of persons and places, and of selected subjects. Minor places are in or near the Kingtons, unless stated otherwise.